100 Things Awesome Teachers Do

By William Emeny

About the Author

William Emeny is a secondary school maths teacher working in the South of England. He has a passion for using ICT to enhance student learning and leads his department in this area. William runs the popular maths teaching resource and ideas blog, *Great Maths Teaching Ideas* (http://www.greatmathsteachingideas.com) that receives over 150,000 visits a year.

Before going into teaching, William worked as a Structural Design Engineer for the prestigious engineering consultancy, Arup. Prior to this, he attained a First Class Masters Degree in Civil Engineering from the University of Exeter.

When not teaching, William enjoys spending time with his family, reading, writing and online blogging. Feel free to get in touch with William online in any of the following ways:

Email: williamgeorgeemeny@gmail.com

Google+:
https://plus.google.com/u/0/111288446773159834123

Twitter: @Maths_Master

Linked In: http://www.linkedin.com/pub/william-emeny/33/ba2/b33

Dedication

To my wonderful wife who makes all the sacrifices to let me pursue what I love doing every day, thank you again. To my parents who taught me what hard work really is, thank you. To my beautiful daughters who keep me young at heart, thank you. To all the amazing teachers who helped me grow through the difficult teenage years, thank you. This book is for you all.

License Notes

Contents

Introduction

If a doctor, lawyer, or a dentist had 40 people in his office at one time, all of whom had different needs, and some of whom didn't want to be there and were causing trouble, and the doctor, lawyer, or dentist, without assistance, had to treat them all with professional excellence for nine months, then he might have some conception of the classroom teacher's job.

Donald D. Quinn

It's been a fantastic day. You feel inspired to try out this new teaching strategy that you've just learned about. Your mind is frantically buzzing about how it could be 'the key' which opens up a whole new world of learning to one of your disengaged pupils.

Ok, maybe you're not quite so keen as that, but you're not the kind of person who views all INSET training days as learning how to suck eggs. You're a teacher who's in the job for the right reasons and you're committed to being a good one. You're willing to take on ideas when you think they are good ones and running with them to improve your own teaching. You're humble enough to admit that you don't know it all.

There's just one problem.

Despite having the very best of intentions, tomorrow 'real life' will take over again. Real life, where you've got to finish marking those exam papers, prepare six lessons for the next day and finish doing your Year 10 reports. That new idea will have to wait. Ultimately it never seems to become the priority because, despite the potential long-term benefits, the short-term fact is that it will take time to prepare for and introduce it; time you just don't have. Ultimately it goes on the pile of 'great ideas that I'll do one day', along with all the other good pieces of advice people have given you over the years to help you become a better teacher.

Maybe it's a brilliant idea and one that you do have time to introduce. You run with it for a couple of weeks before it becomes a little stale and you move on. You promise yourself to resurrect it in the future when it's time for a change again. Will you remember a year down the line? When you're feeling a bit rusty and samey and you're looking for a change, will you remember it? Maybe. Maybe not. If you're like me then probably not. What a waste!

I feel like this person on a daily basis. There's nothing worse than letting a good idea drift off your radar, never to be retrieved. If this predicament describes you then you've made an excellent choice by buying this book. Well done!

Now you own this book, if you every find yourself with a moment to spare and looking for a good idea to try out, speed through pages to find something that you want to give a try and go for it! You see, this book was written for those moments when you're feeling stale and boring as a teacher and you want some inspiration. Think of it as a *bullet list of things to try out* when you want to keep both your own and your pupils' motivation up. If you stored these ideas in your head you'd probably forget them over time, but now you've got this book, you can go searching for a new idea anytime in the safe knowledge that they will still be here sitting on these pages ready and waiting for you.

Have you ever watched one of your colleagues teach? If not, why not?! I find it a totally liberating experience. Whenever I watch one of my colleagues teach I always walk away with something brand new in my mind to try out with my own classes. It may be a new way to introduce a topic, a behaviour management strategy or just some reassurance that despite feeling like the world (or just all the kids) are against me somedays, other colleagues are facing the same challenges. I have always found watching a colleague teach to be a positive experience and I honestly believe it's the best INSET you can get.

Nonetheless, I promise that the moment you ask your fellow teacher if they'd mind if you just sat quietly in the back of their room to get some new ideas you will be met with one of the following phrases in a pained, self-conscious, caught-on-the-hop voice:

"Err, yeah if you want to but be aware this is going to be a bit of a dull one today"

"Sure, but it's not going to be anything special, just textbooks today I'm afraid"

The first time someone asked if they could informally come to watch me I caught myself doing the same! Why are teachers so defensive? It's a lonely job most of the time (in terms of adult-to-adult interaction) so why are we so anxious when a colleague wants to see you do what you're good at, what you're paid to do? I think it's to do with the 'formal observation' system. The OFSTED directed criteria where you have to pull off an 'outstanding' lesson at a specified time with a specified class. I don't want to get bogged down in thoughts about this system of being able to pull the rabbit out of the hat when it really matters except to say that I think it's much more important what's going on in your classroom on a day-by-day basis, what the average quality of learning is rather than in a one-off lesson. In a job where many of the factors that influence the learning of your pupils are outside of your control, I suppose it makes sense that teachers are defensive when they get told to pull an outstanding one out of the bag on Friday period 5 just after a wet and windy lunchtime.

Why am I mentioning all this? I want to be clear that this book is not about tips for producing an outstanding one-off lesson that OFSTED would drool over. This book is about pragmatic, tried and tested strategies for improving the quality of learning in your classroom on a daily basis. This book aims to promote a *culture of outstanding* and one that remains valid even when OFSTED change their outstanding criteria yet again.

Given all that has just been said about teachers' defensiveness, it does take some guts to stand up and say 'X is a good idea'. What is a good idea to one teacher is a poor one to another. We all teach differently because you can't do this job well without your personality shining through. Therefore, as we are all human (I hope), and all different, I can't promise you that you'll find every idea in this book life-changingly brilliant, but I can say that they have been shared with me by people I respect as being in the know; people doing the job in the classroom rather than those telling others how to do it from the sidelines. Each idea makes sense to me as something that I could incorporate into my own practice for the benefit of my pupils' learning and I hope you feel the same way about many of them too.

You won't find me referencing lots of academic literature in this book. I do fully understand the view that if you are saying 'research has shown', it needs to be backed up by references. However, I don't want that for this book. Whilst I have huge respect for the academic field, I am a practising teacher who does not have time to read the minutiae of details, assumptions and context behind every piece of academic research. 'Would it work for me?' is the only question I am concerned with. Please don't think I'm not wanting to give credit to the highly skilled and invaluable academic scholars out there. They do really great work and deserve their recognition where it is due. They push the boundaries of our understanding. However, this is not a book where an academic is telling you about research findings that improve learning in theory. Rather, I want you to think of it as one teacher talking to another, sharing things they have found that work for them. If some of it has come from academic research then great, if other parts have come from the *University of Life and Experience* then that is as worthwhile too in my opinion so long as it works. With the internet and online journals available almost ubiquitously now you can find detailed research publications if you'd like to read in more depth on a topic. I personally don't get much time to do so and I'm sure you don't too if you are a full time teacher. Thus you'll find in this book I may say 'research has found' without fully referencing it. If this enrages and disgusts you please feel free to read one of the more academic based teaching books. Otherwise, if you are interested in the sharing of good ideas from one teacher to another as we would over a cup of tea at breaktime then read on!

I'm not the world's best or most experienced teacher but I do want to be the best one I can. It's a journey and I'm learning every day. I'm glad you're on this journey with me. This book shares the best bits I've learned so far. I hope you learn something new and feel inspired to try it out in your own classroom.

William Emeny

Disclaimer: Please note, all views and opinions expressed in this book are my own and are not necessarily those of my employer. I have made considerable effort to ensure all the information in this book is factually correct, but in the case that I have got something wrong, please let me know and I will be happy to correct it in a future edition of the book. Thank you.

~***~

Lesson Planning

The task of the excellent teacher is to stimulate "apparently ordinary" people to unusual effort. The tough problem is not in identifying winners: it is in making winners out of ordinary people.

K. Patricia Cross

Idea 1- Concentrate on the learning, not the teaching

When I started teaching I spent a lot of time creating worksheets, presentations and other resources. Whilst I hadn't identified my motivation in these terms at the time, I was creating resources pursuing the belief that to be a better teacher you needed to be able to explain things better. If teachers were the givers of knowledge, then the best ones were those that conveyed it the best, ideally with a charismatic, engaging personality. Naive? Yes!

Whilst being able to explain ideas well is certainly an important part of the job, pupils can be totally engaged and engrossed in a presentation or an activity without learning anything. **Edutainment is not learning**.

I learned quickly that if you use only teacher-led lessons where you spend a significant proportion of the time explaining, demonstrating and ultimately, talking at the pupils, everything that they learn will have come through you. You are the funnel through which all knowledge is disseminated and acquired, and ultimately this is a very inefficient method of learning. How many teachers complain about how poor students are as independent learners yet give them five hours a day of being talked at? As teachers, we have all been trained to differentiate in our lessons to cater for pupils of varying attainment but this is very hard in a traditional teacher-led lesson. No matter what you do, if you have pupils of different attainment in your class, a 'chalk-and-talk' lesson will be pitched too quickly for some of your pupils and too slowly for others. If you are skilled then maybe you'll get the balance 'right' and have a 50/50 split! I'm sure the one pupil 'in-the-middle' made excellent progress!

These days I know, particularly when I teach a topic that some pupils in the class will have some previous knowledge of, that more learning takes place if the pupils are working on questions and challenges much earlier on than I traditionally would have given them. Let their intuition guide them on questions to get them engaged in a topic. If they get stuck, asking their peers is often sufficient to get a correct answer and if it's not we can always pause the lesson for a mini 'pitstop' where they ask me to explain something to the class. They are so much more engaged if they come up with the question that asks me to explain something because it relates directly to solving a problem they have in their hands. It's learning through doing rather than learning by being passive.

How this idea relates to your subject and your teaching will be very personal to you. How you incorporate it into your own teaching will take some thought and creativity. All the generality that I can share here is that when you look at a planned lesson, take the opportunities to reduce the amount of time you spend presenting and explaining and get the pupils into the activities sooner. It develops their intuition, problem solving skills and improves engagement.

It's the learning that counts, not the teaching, and learning doesn't have to just come through you.

Idea 2- Use Bloom's Taxonomy. It's good. Really good

I'm not fan of making things any more complex than they need to be and also I dislike edu-jargon. That said, Bloom's Taxonomy does give a nice structure to think about progression in your lessons and how to get your pupils to really learn a topic well.

In 1956 Benjamin Bloom chaired a committee of educators who published Taxonomy of educational objectives: the classification of educational goals. The original taxonomy focussed on three 'domains': cognitive, affective and psychomotor corresponding to different areas of intelligence. The cognitive domain is of particular interest to most teachers and looked like this:

Original Bloom's Taxonomy:

Evaluation

Synthesis

Analysis

Application

Comprehension

Knowledge

The idea is that all cognitive learning is based on this hierarchy. The most basic type of cognitive learning is knowledge and the types of learning rise in difficulty and complexity up to evaluation. The taxonomy is based on the assumption that you cannot climb up the pyramid until you are competent in the types of learning below any given level. For example you can't **analyse** the similarities and differences between red dwarf, white dwarf or neutron stars until you have the **knowledge** of what they are, the **comprehension** of that knowledge and the ability to **apply** it to solve problems.

Bloom's Taxonomy was revised in 2000 by Lorin Anderson, a former student of Bloom. The two significant changes were the swapping of evaluation and synthesis in the order of the hierarchy and the changing of the names from nouns to verbs. In my opinion the verb-form of Bloom's Taxonomy is much more user-friendly and easier to apply to your own lesson planning.

Revised Bloom's Taxonomy:

Creating

Evaluating

Analysing

Applying

Understanding

Remembering

To assist in applying Bloom's Revised Taxonomy to your own lesson planning here are some key words that can be used to guide the creation of questions or activities that correspond to each category in the hierarchy:

Creating- compose, create, devise, design, generate, modify, plan, reconstruct, reorganise, revise, rewrite, summarise

Evaluating- appraise, compare, criticise, conclude, defend, describe, evaluate, justify, interpret, relate, decide

Analysing- break down, analyse, identify, infer, outline, select, separate

Applying- compute, calculate, demonstrate, modify, operate, predict, prepare, produce, solve, apply

Understanding- convert, estimate, explain, generalise, explain

Remembering- describe, identify, label, list, match, name, recall, select

I find the real usefulness of Bloom's Revised Taxonomy to come when I think about planning progression across a few lessons. The activities I give pupils on a topic rise through the levels in Bloom's Revised Taxonomy. So for example, pupils learning about straight edge and compass constructions in my maths lessons might learn to **remember** what angle bisectors and perpendicular bisectors are, then **understand** how to construct them. They may then **apply** this knowledge to drawing inscribed and circumscribed circles. Then they could **analyse** why the series of prescribed actions to construct the bisectors produce the geometric results they do. They could then look at angle bisectors of angles close to 180 degrees and **evaluate** the similarities and differences of those with perpendicular bisector constructions before finally **creating** their own investigations into perpendicular and angle bisectors of sides and angles of regular and non-regular polygons respectively.

This is just an example and in real life I often don't cover every level of the hierarchy as there is often not time to do so. I do find it a useful guide however for planning progression through a topic and also, importantly, a reminder to challenge students regularly with the types of task associated with the higher tiers of the taxonomy. It reminds me that you can't say a pupil has learned something just because they can remember it. I guess it does raise an interesting question of how high up the taxonomy a pupil needs to climb with a concept before they can consider it learned? I don't have an answer to that but an interesting exercise a colleague of mine once did was to see where the GCSE grade criteria for various subjects would sit on the taxonomy. Sure enough the A and A* grades were associated with synthesis and evaluation of information whereas the lower grades were just associated with remembering and comprehending knowledge.

Being aware of Bloom's Revised Taxonomy when planning a series of lessons is certainly useful in guiding your choices of activities across a topic. I recommend it highly!

Idea 3- Same starter and plenary

My current headteacher always comes out with three questions after doing a formal lesson observation. What did you want them to learn? What did they learn? How do you know? Consider using the same starter and plenary as a great way to show yourself, your pupils and any observers what pupils have learned through your lesson.

You really have to get the pitch right and think about your question carefully when you use this technique. Link the question directly to the learning objective. If you wanted the pupils to learn about the formation of oxbow lakes you might show an aerial view of one and ask how do you think this lake was formed? Get the pupils to write down their ideas. As the plenary to the lesson show the same picture and question and get pupils to write their new answer next to what they wrote in the starter. This then clearly shows you as their teacher and the pupils themselves what they have learned during the lesson.

Idea 4- The hook. Grab their attention early

Rather than "Today we are learning about the works of Pablo Picasso", how about "If he thought women had ears in the middle of their face and noses on the side of their heads, why was Picasso such a great painter?"

Instead of "Today we are learning how to add fractions", why not use "If I score 6 out of 10 on a test and 8 out of 10 on another I got 14 out of 20. Why is 6/10 + 8/10 not equal to 14/20?".

"Today we are learning about the human respiratory system" or "How much oxygen would a spaceship need to carry to get a person to Mars and back safely?". Which lesson would you rather sit in if you were 12 years old?!

A thought-provoking lesson title on the board as they walk through the door gets them engaged early. Making the lesson objective a question rather than a statement is good advice. On a good day they're even talking about the question with their mates whilst they unpack their bags!

Idea 5- 'What did I want you to learn today?'

A nice plenary to use now and again is to ask your pupils "What did I want you to learn today?" This is most effective if you haven't given your lesson objectives at the start of the lesson otherwise you just get the lesson objective recited with little thought on behalf of the pupils.

This is a great way to find out if they have learned what you intended them to and often turns up some surprises. Sometimes it is nice to get the pupils to answer this question individually in their books and then do a sharing session with the class. Other times you can get the whole class to brainstorm all their answers on a whiteboard and then have a class discussion about it.

"What did I want you to learn today?" also gets them to go through the valuable process of reflecting on their learning. Following it up with "What could I use this new knowledge for?" gets them thinking about applications of their new knowledge, giving it meaning which helps memory retention.

Idea 6- If rushed for time, just plan your questions

Teachers are very busy people and often something has to give. Now and again we all find ourselves short of time when lesson planning and thus coming up with the best possible plan in the short time available is a skill every teacher needs in their armory.

Some advice I read once was, 'If you can only do one thing when planning your lessons, plan your questions'. The argument is that some good questions can form the basis of a brilliant lesson that is engaging, inspiring and thought-provoking. Activities and tasks can be written up on the board and made up on the spot if required but good questions often require more thought and often don't flow freely on the spot in a lesson.

Questions that are open, allowing different, but valid answers are often much more engaging than closed questions with right or wrong answers. 'Tell me as many mathematical things you can about this set of numbers: 12, 32, 3, 45 and 44' is much more thought-provoking than 'How many of these numbers are prime?'.

Idea 7- Share your resources, reap what you sow

You get back what you give in lots of situations in life and sharing resources is certainly one of them. Get into the habit of sharing your good lesson ideas and resources with your colleagues and I promise you'll get some good ones back in return. It's a great way of keeping fresh and understanding that there is more than one way to teach a topic.

There's a lot of job satisfaction to be gained when you know other people are using resources you've created. It doesn't have to stop with your colleagues. There are many sites on the internet that make your resources free to teachers the world over. I upload a lot of mine to the Times Educational Supplement website and get a real buzz when someone is positive about the resource I uploaded. You never know what it can lead to… On the back of me being a regular resource uploaded I got a free invite to the Times Educational Supplement School Awards hosted by the comedian Rory Bremner in 2011 and had lovely day meeting lots of amazing educators at the Hilton Hotel, Park Lane, London! Some good websites for downloading free teaching resources from are:

The Times Educational Supplement: http://www.tes.co.uk/

Teaching Ideas: http://www.teachingideas.co.uk/

Guardian Teacher Network: http://teachers.guardian.co.uk

Primary Resources: http://www.primaryresources.co.uk/

Ngfl Cymru: http://www.ngfl-cymru.org.uk/vtc-home.htm

Idea 8- Learn how to search for resources, don't reinvent the wheel

I remember in my teacher training year as feeling like my life had to go on hold as the course consumed every waking minute. Looking back I remember feeling like I had to make a resource for every lesson that I taught. The amount of time I spent creating resources was considerable and, in hindsight, totally unnecessary.

The internet is now an absolutely fantastic place to search for resources. Whether you do a straight Google search or you use one of the many sites that collect resources in a single place and make them available by topic, you really don't need to be making resources that often.

The majority of the resources I use are also free to download and whilst there are plenty of websites out there that will sell you resources, I think with some time invested in finding the best sites you will see that high quality free resources are out there and they are faster to find than to make.

Idea 9- Get blogging and get social

On the last day of my teacher training course we had a session at the university where all of my trainee colleagues met and had to give a five minute 'this resource worked for me' presentation. The quality of the resources that my peers had created was very high and I left that session buzzing with enthusiasm and a notebook full of wonderful new teaching ideas and resources. From that day on I committed to regularly sharing teaching resources. I set up a blog called *Great Maths Teaching Ideas* (http://www.greatmathsteachingideas.com) to share maths teaching ideas and resources, which in 18 months grew to receiving over 500 visits a day. Sounds like a lot of work; it was! However, I honestly believe I have reaped more than I have sown. I encouraged my blog visitors to connect with me on social networks such as Twitter, Facebook and Google+. Within 18 months I had a network of 2900 Twitter followers, 600 Facebook followers and 500 Google+ followers, the majority of whom were practicing teachers. I could post a question such as "Has anyone got an interesting way of teaching cumulative frequency?" and within minutes I would have suggestions from teachers around the world. The blog was a powerful way of connecting with people and building a network of similar minded people but the real benefits to my own teaching came through the interactions I had, and still do have with other teaching professionals on the social networks.

Creating your own blog isn't difficult. There are many free websites that you can do this on. One of the best in my opinion is Blogger (http://www.blogger.com). If you just want to connect with other teachers to share ideas you certainly can do it without creating a blog. My advice would be to search for the blogs of other teachers and then connect with them via the links on their websites. Once you are connected with a few teachers and sharing ideas you will be surprised by how fast your network can grow.

Idea 10- Plan with the teachers of classes 'next to' your own

You shouldn't need to reinvent the wheel in terms of resources but why do it with lesson planning either? If you teach in a good-sized school and your classes are set by ability then there will no doubt be an overlap in the ability of pupils in your own class and those in the classes above and below your own. If you want to save time planning great lessons then why not share the planning load with the teachers of those other classes?

Often you'll find that sharing planning takes more time than you'd think to begin with but then it really starts to pay off. Not only is a problem shared a problem halved but there is something about knowing that your colleague is going to be relying some of your planning that makes you focus on producing a great lesson. When sharing your plan with them it does encourage conversations about different ways to teach topics which improves your own practice. Halve your planning and learn some new ideas... Two for one!

~***~

Learning Styles

If we teach today as we taught yesterday we rob our children of tomorrow.

John Dewey

Idea 11- VAK your lessons

The *Theory of Multiple Intelligences* formed by Howard Gardner is well-known to most teachers and so I will only summarise the main ideas here. If it's totally new to you get on the internet and you'll find plenty of detailed information about the theory.

Gardner came up with seven criteria for a behaviour to be classified as an 'intelligence'. These were:

1. Potential for brain isolation by brain damage,

2. Place in evolutionary history,

3. Presence of core operations,

4. Susceptibility to encoding (symbolic expression)

5. A distinct developmental progression

6. The existence of savants, prodigies and other exceptional people,

7. Support from experimental psychology and psychometric findings.

He believed that eight abilities meet these criteria and are therefore 'intelligences':

1. Logical- mathematical

2. Spatial

3. Linguistic

4. Bodily- kinesthetic

5. Musical

6. Interpersonal

7. Intrapersonal

8. Naturalistic

His research found that being ‘strong’ in one intelligence didn’t necessarily mean you would be ‘strong’ in others. There is naturally debate about the detail of this framework for defining different kinds of intelligence but I believe from a teacher’s point of view it is a useful structure to help us plan lessons for learners with different preferred learning styles.

Think back to a day-to-day lesson you gave recently. How many preferred learning styles did it support? Research has shown that we as teachers tend to teach the majority of the time in the learning style that we personally prefer. Do you? I confess to being guilty here and have to remind myself regularly that there are other styles!

It is unreasonable to plan for all the learning styles in every lesson. All we can realistically aim for is a regular mixture. To simplify things even further I have heard of teachers who ‘**VAK**’ their lesson plans. The idea is that when putting a lesson plan together think to yourself ‘have

I catered for the **V**isual, **A**udible and **K**inesthetic learners?'. If you have then that is a reasonable approach that will be successful in helping all learners with their different preferred learning styles.

Whether you try to regularly address the preferred learning styles of different learners using a multiple intelligences or a VAK framework is entirely up to you but the core idea of ensuring you regularly have a mix in your lessons is important. The top-set pupils are often the ones who learn well from 'chalk-and-talk' lessons. Are they in the top set because this is the regular diet they get and thus only the passive learners happy to sit and listen to six Powerpoints a day are the ones that are most 'successful'? Don't let it be the case!

Idea 12- Mnemonics and songs

Sing to the tune of 'Pop Goes The Weasel':

Multiply the length by the width,

Gives the area of a rectangle.

Base times height divided by two,

Is the area of a triangle.

Half the sum of the parallel sides,

Times the distance between them.

That's the way you calculate,

The area of a trapezium.

When you want to know the speed of light, count the number of letters in each word of this sentence:

We guarantee certainty, clearly referring to this light mnemonic

299,792,458 m/sec

Kings and Queens of England:

Willy, Willy, Harry, Steve,

Harry, Dick, John, Harry Three;

One, two, three Neds, Richard Two,

Harries Four Five Six, then who?

Edwards Four Five, Dick the Bad,

Harries (twain) Ned Six (the lad);

Mary, Bessie, James ye ken,

Then Charlie, Charlie, James again

Will and Mary, Anna Gloria

Georges four, Will Fourth, Victoria

Edward Seven next, and then

Came George the Fifth in nineteen ten

Ned the Eighth soon abdicated

Then George the Sixth was coronated

After which Elizabeth

And that's all folks until her death

The internet is a great place to find mnemonics for your subject to keep your audible learners learning. If you can't find one about a specific topic why not put the kids' creative minds to the task of creating one?

Idea 13- Use visual aids

This advice is ages old but good. If you're doing a lesson about the respiratory system, there is nothing like seeing a pair of pigs lungs on the table. If you were teaching about the World Wars, bring in some artifacts that bring the topic to life.

Using a visual aid when teaching definitely adds to your pupils engagement with the topic. They make the lesson contextual and also, in my opinion, provide an anchor in pupils memory which they can refer to later. You can always refer back to the lesson as 'remember that time I brought in the ...?'.

Using visual aids can make for a great starter to a lesson by presenting the objects and asking pupils what they think the lesson is going to be about. If the visual aid is metaphorical rather than explicit, then this approach can be even more engaging. For example, you could ask questions like 'how is this sword similar to Winston Churchill?' or 'what is the similarity between this magnifying glass and human eye?'.

You don't need to stop at tangible, hand-held objects though. Flash cards, costumes, pictures and charts can all be used as a effective visual aids.

Idea 14- Use colour

You can use colour in different ways, whether you are highlighting key facts and vocabulary that you want to stand out from the page or board, or using it to categorise information or classify it, colour is a very effective tool that some of us often forget to use. Get your pupils into the habit of highlighting and classifying information using colour.

If a picture speaks a thousand words then I believe colour is an important half-way medium between the two which enhances the communicative power of the written word.

Idea 15- iPods for recording notes and podcasting

Lots of kids have mobile computing devices in their pockets these days. Many of these devices, such as iPod Touchs, have free applications which allow you to record audio or video notes. For your audible learners, why not get them to record their notes on their iPod so that they can then revise by listening back to them? For your visual learners, get them to record video tutorials that they make themselves to revise key concepts.

Whilst these tools are very powerful to help individual learners revise, I think they really come into their own when they start sharing their productions. There is lots of freely available software on the internet that allows your pupils to create, produce and then distribute their podcasts. One such program is Audacity which is free to download from http://audacity.sourceforge.net/. Don't worry if you don't instinctively know how to use these programs. I assure you your students will and they can even teach you!

Why not to split up the syllabus and give each learner in your class a part of it? They could then create audio or video podcasts which could all be put onto a single website that would help everyone in the class revise all the key concepts across the whole syllabus! I find giving kids responsibility over their own part of a big project like this to be good for motivation as if they don't complete the work they let the whole class down. They also learn the value of teamwork and what can be achieved when lots of people all pull in one direction.

My main advice about using mobile devices to record audio or video podcasts is don't let the technology put you off. The kids will find a technological solution that works if you give them that task. Don't feel that because you don't understand the technology, the kids won't. Treat it as a trial and error exercise and I think you'll be pleased with the results.

Idea 16- Isolate the senses

A wonderful teacher once said to me that they feel kids are losing their ability to listen. Personally, I think she's right. Kids are constantly bombarded with all manner of audible and visual stimuli these days and many of them cannot sit down and fully listen to something. If it's not both audible and visual as a stimulus and fast paced then many kids seem unable to pay attention for any extended period of time.

Let's not fall into the trap of blaming the kids here though. Their DNA is the same as ours and they are only a product of the society in which they are living. I do think that there is an upside to this however. Try this simple task. Put the television on and turn it onto a news channel. Rather than sitting there watching and listening to it as you normally would, close your eyes and just listen to the news. Do you notice how instantly you seem to be concentrating more on the story and focusing on it than you normally would? Now isolate your hearing sense by turning the volume to mute. Try to decipher what is being said in the story to see if you can follow it by just looking at it with your eyes. Once again you really have to pay attention if you want to follow it.

I haven't read any research to back this up but from personal experience in the classroom I find that if you force the kids to isolate one of their senses it can help with their concentration if you want them to focus on something for an extended period of time. Demonstrate a concept on the board without talking about it. Explain a concept in class but get the learners to close their eyes whilst they are listening to it. In a world where there have never been more distraction temptations I find that getting pupils to isolate their senses and just use one at a time can help with their concentration on learning new ideas.

Idea 17- Infographics

Do you know what *infographics* are? They are great tools for learning! An infographic is a poster that contains interesting information about a topic. They are usually based around giving key facts or statistics about the topic and often contain lots of graphs and charts. Forget gaudy Microsoft Excel produced bar charts though, the graphs and charts in infographics are produced by graphic designers who really care about making the information beautiful. A good infographic is as visually appealing as it is informative.

Infographics are freely available all over the internet. One very good site where you can access high quality infographics about a whole range of topics is http://www.good.is/infographics. From *The Fantasy Sports Economy* to *How Does Lack of Water Affect Women and Children?*, this website has infographics for a whole range of topics including news, business, culture, design, lifestyle and technology that are all freely available to download.

Infographics are a great way to start a topic. They often highlight key ideas, interesting trends, with the benefits of the information being right up-to-date. Giving groups of pupils an infographic to analyse is often a very engaging activity. Give them some questions which can be answered by interpreting the infographic and this helps support their engagement further.

Once both you and your pupils are familiar with infographics you can then set them the task of creating their own to summarise a topic. Teachers have been asking pupils to create posters for years, but call it an infographic and encourage them to follow visually appealing styles such as those on infographics that you find on the internet, and suddenly they seems so much more engaged!

Idea 18- Manipulatives

Fantastic for kinesthetic learners, manipulatives are objects that assist learning. They can take many forms including card sorts, flash cards or objects with specific functions such as hundreds, tens and units apparatus or simply coins of money in maths. Their main purpose is to improve conceptual understanding but can also be used to stimulate higher-order thinking processes, often through categorising information.

I am personally a big fan of card sorts. You can use them for different purposes such a recalling knowledge, prioritisation and categorisation.

Card sorts can simply contain a series of questions and answers that pupils have to match up, domino fashion to practice recalling some knowledge. On the tougher questions pupils quite often get involved in discussions to eliminate certain answers which in itself develops their problem solving skills.

Asking students to order their cards into a 'diamond nine' is a nice card sort activity if you want them to prioritise information. For example, you might like them to 'use a diamond nine to sort the importance of events in causing World War I'. They then have to form this formation with the cards:

Card 1

Card 2 Card 3

Card 4 Card 5 Card 6

Card 7 Card 8

Card 9

The idea is that they place the most important event in the Card 1 position and the least important in the Card 9 position, graduating between the extremes in between. You could ask pupils to do this by writing them down from a list on the board but from personal experience of doing these card sorts myself, being able to hold and manipulate the cards frees up the trial and error nature of the task and seems to allow people to focus on specific items at a time as they hold them in their hands.

Using card sorts to facilitate pupils classifying information is also an effective activity. You can either tell pupils what categories you'd like the cards sorted in to or allow them to invent their own. I often find the later approach a useful one as it results in class discussions about what categories they chose and why, which in itself is an interesting exercise.

As the world becomes ever-more virtual, online manipulatives become more available. There are many websites on the internet that provide virtual card sorts where pupils can drag-and-drop the cards.

Moving away from card sorts, other virtual manipulatives exist online in a variety of forms. Examples include simulations where you can increase and decrease the temperature of a material to see the effect on the vibration and physical states of the atoms of that material, and interactive geometry webpages where you can learn angle facts by clicking and dragging points on a shape around. Perhaps the best virtual manipulative I have seen is the freely downloadable *Google Earth* software. Pupils literally have the world in their hands and can zoom in to any spot on the planet with amazing resolution.

All these fantastic resources are out there just waiting for you. Get Google-ing and you'll be surprised what you can find!

Idea 19- Acting out

Learning Shakespeare at school was a painful experience for me. I found the language difficult and spent so much time focusing on how to interpret the meaning of the phrases that I couldn't seem to 'get the flow' of the play. I found the humour difficult to grasp, and let's face it, a joke isn't funny if you have to explain it! I will never forget the difficulty I had with the language and interpretation of Shakespeare's works as a child. However, I see this as a very positive experience as I have an appreciation of some of the language learning difficulties that some of the leaners in my classroom have.

These days I love reading, watching and listening to Shakespeare. It all hinged on the first time that I saw it performed live. I was fortunate enough to visit The Globe and sit in the gallery to watch a performance of one of the plays. I understood the jokes and was amazed by how relevant they still were to modern society. They were as funny then as they would have been 400 years ago. By seeing the context of the play through the acting somehow my difficulties with the language seemed to evaporate. The written word is a powerful way to communicate but even more so if body language accompanies it.

This experience made me realise that as a teacher I should have pupils acting out concepts and ideas as a strategy in my teaching armoury. If pupils find an idea difficult could acting it out help? This doesn't need to only be for literary masterpieces. Any story could be adapted to acting out and indeed many other things too. I have seen PE lessons where pupils move through a large virtual heart on the floor simulating blood flow, science lessons where pupils pretend to be individual electrons moving around a circuit and maths lessons where pupils have to stand in places according to rules to demonstrate the idea of loci. The possibilities are endless and I think we should take every opportunity possible to do this kind of learning as pupils always say to me how they find it easy to remember what you are trying to get them to learn.

Idea 20- Story telling

Kids are creative. By the last year of secondary school their creativity seems to wane and I think this is because the 'creativity muscle' isn't being exercised enough. I am a big fan of creative activities to enhance learning as I feel they motivate pupils by allowing them to express themselves yet doing so around a concept that you want them to learn.

Humans are very good at remembering stories. We read lots of short stories to our young children, often with a moral emphasis. In the story 'The Boy Who Called Wolf' children learn about the negative consequences of lying but they do so in a way that is very engaging and that they will remember.

Bringing storytelling into your lessons, either from you introducing or explaining a topic, or by pupils consolidating their knowledge by writing their own creative story about a topic, is a super way to enhance learning. In my own subject of mathematics I take every opportunity that I can to talk about the history of the topic. Whilst some of mathematics is very dry, the history and story about the development of the concept is often a lot more interesting! Would this be applicable to your subject?

~***~

Learning Environment

Education is not the filling of a pail, but the lighting of a fire.

William Butler Yeats

Idea 21- Plants in the classroom

It has been found in studies that putting plants in an indoor environment has many benefits. These are alleged to be increased productivity, reduced stress and blood pressure, and improved air quality through the reduction in particulate matter. Feel free to dive into the details of the research if you feel you need to, but I believe there to be something very beneficial in bringing a bit of nature into your classroom.

Idea 22- Natural lighting

You may have very little or no control of the lighting in your classroom, but if you do have any control whatsoever, you should definitely maximise the use of natural, rather than artificial lighting. In particular, reduce the use of fluorescent lighting if at all possible. Studies have shown over-illumination or the unnatural spectral composition of artificial lighting can cause measurable negative health effects such as headaches, fatigue, increased blood pressure and increased anxiety. How unhelpful for learning! I don't think these results are surprising. It is only within the last 140 years that we have had artificial electric lighting and thus people have spent most of their time on earth relying on natural light. If at all possible maximise the use of natural lighting in your classroom.

Idea 23- It's getting hot, hot, hot

Whilst your control may be limited, I would encourage you to do all you can to provide a comfortable temperature within your classroom. Use everything that is available to you. Get fans running and open windows and your classroom door if things get warm. You can also get a reflective, translucent film that can be stuck on windows that receive a lot of direct sun to reduce the amount of heat entering your classroom. Try using humidifiers if the school will fund them to reduce the air moisture content on a hot summer day. Remind pupils to take their blazers/ jumpers off.

If you have the choice, prefer to have your classroom a little cool rather than a little warm. Pupils seem to continue to learn well if a little cold but nearly all become sluggish if warm which really affects the learning in a bad way.

Idea 24- Music in the classroom

Using music in the classroom seems to be taboo with many teachers. Why?! Music is designed to cause an emotional response and you can use it to 'steer' your pupils into an emotional and mental state that is good for learning.

Through improving your DJing skills, you can get a excitable class to settle down and focus or an apathetic class to switch on. My advice is to give it more than one lesson to see the benefits. Being 'the teacher who plays music whilst we work' is quite a novelty at the beginning and pupils love to express their views about what you should be playing, but once that wears off I find that the music has more of an effect in getting the emotional response in the pupils that you would like. Experiment with genres of music to see what works for you and your pupils.

Rather than playing music to the whole class, consider letting pupils listen to their iPods or other music players through their headphones. Particularly if you have a class with pupils that like to distract each other, you may find that this strategy is a good one for getting them to focus on their own work individually.

Idea 25- Keep it fresh

Consider purchasing an air freshener or two for your classroom. Quite often you don't recognise the unpleasant whiff if you have been sitting in your classroom for an hour with some Year 8s that had PE in the rain the lesson before, but I promise your next class will notice it immediately when they arrive! Getting pupils in the right frame of mind for learning is about making them feel comfortable in their environment. If they walk into your classroom and get a whiff of lemon rather than of *eau de sweaty boy* they are more likely to want to stay (and then hopefully learn)!

Idea 26- Pictures make the place a home from home

There are two schools of thought on this point so I'll leave it up to you to decide if you think this one is appropriate for your particular classes.

The idea is that putting up a few pictures of your pupils and some of their best work gives them a feeling that they 'own' the classroom too. It's meant to create a 'homely and welcoming' environment where pupils will be more relaxed and inclined to look after the room and the equipment. You can give pupils the responsibility for maintaining their class' display to further this idea. Tell them they can add to the display at break or lunchtimes and they can decide what pictures they'd like to put up and what work they'd like to display.

I am fully aware that many people would dismiss this idea saying that the state of most teenagers' bedrooms would testify to the fact that giving them their own space doesn't encourage them to look after it! Many others would also say that it is vital that pupils get a clear message that the teacher owns the room and everything in it for behaviour management purposes. I think which way you go on this idea depends on what the pupils you teach are like, but I have met teachers who really believe in it.

Idea 27- Rows, groups, individually spaced? What about a 'U'?

Rows, groups or individually spaced? What about a 'U' shape so you can easily get around to each pupil? The way you arrange the tables and desks in your room has a great effect on the behaviour of the pupils. Groups of desks certainly does promote talking between pupils but this may be exactly what you want if it is about the work. Rows allows for easier behaviour management with each pupil facing you but it can be difficult to get to pupils on the middle of rows if they need help. The 'U' shape works only if you've got space for it.

I've met teachers who insist on all these seating arrangements. The best advice is to experiment and see what works for you and your teaching style. Give each arrangement that you try time so that the novelty wears off and you can more accurately assess its impact on learning in the longer term.

Idea 28- Inspirational quotes

I would much rather pupils left school with a real thirst for knowledge than feeling like they'd learned everything we'd taught them. What morals and principles will they choose to live their life by? I think we must never underestimate our effect on informing their choices.

One of my teachers at school had Ghandi's famous quote *Be the change you want to see in the world* displayed prominently in their classroom. I've never forgotten it and it always seems to pop into my mind whenever I'm feeling aggrieved about something. It is still informing my decisions over a decade on.

You may never know the effect they have on your pupils, but putting up some inspirational quotes around your classroom could help them make some good decisions about how they want to live their life.

Idea 29- Key facts posters

Repetition is the key for deep learning of key facts and information. If you place some posters up around your teaching room and department showing key facts pupils will see them each day. In my own subject of maths, I have found this technique to be beneficial, especially for the more 'dry' things pupils need to remember such as unit conversions like how many metres there are in a kilometre and how many milligrams in gram.

You don't need to create the posters from scratch. Just do an internet search and you'll find countless numbers available for free download.

Idea 30- Nemo, the class pet

Why not get a class pet? Goldfish or hamsters seem to be popular with many teachers as they require relatively little looking after. Make it the responsibility of your tutor group to clean them out and feed them, under your supervision of course!

Having a class pet can relax pupils and make your classroom a space that they really enjoy coming to. There is definitely a natural human tendency to care for things in nature and I think having a class pet can help meet this need. In short, *nurturing nature seems to be natural!*

A teacher once told me about the results of study where they gave some residents in a nursing home a plant to look after. Amazingly, this simple change resulted in the residents who looked after plants living significantly longer. Caring for something in nature has health benefits! I'm not aware of any studies that have replicated this using pets rather than plants but it would seem likely that the benefits could be comparable. Whilst you are not teaching elderly people on a daily basis, try getting a class pet and see what a positive change it can have on your pupils.

~***~

Marking and Feedback

The whole purpose of education is to turn mirrors into windows

Sydney J. Harris

Idea 31- Mark as they go to make the feedback instant

In his fantastic book *Essential Motivation in the Classroom*, Ian Gilbert talks about concentration spans of children and how they have decreased over the years. He argues though, that many boys who show a remarkably short concentration span when working on tasks at school seem to be able to devote many continuous hours to computer games. The 'I can't do it' excuse that some pupils use to not persist with a challenging task in a lesson seems to be somewhat of a misdirection that is inaccurate. The same pupils go home and battle through difficult levels on computer games, having go after go when they fail. Ian Gilbert argues that it is the fact that the **feedback is instant** that encourages the kids to persist with computer games. They know where and why they went wrong the moment they made the mistake and thus learned quickly not to do it again. This is in contrast to them struggling with a homework then it taking a week before they receive the feedback that they got it all wrong.

I am personally a fan of Ian Gilbert's argument but how can we incorporate instant feedback into our lessons to encourage persistence in the pupils? This may not be appropriate for every subject but one thing I find effective is to get the pupils marking their own work as they go. They do three questions then look up the answers (either in the back of the book, on the board, or on another sheet I give them) and mark what they have done. I can't imagine anything more demoralising than doing thirty questions and then finding out that they are all wrong! What a waste of time and you haven't learned anything! If your pupils know within the first few questions that they are going wrong, you can intervene and help them whilst there is still time in the lesson left for them to practice doing it right.

Pupils at first often seem uncomfortable with the idea that you are giving them the answers at the same time as the questions, but after you explain that they need to look at the exercises from a learning perspective rather than a competition to get it all right before they check their answers, they do seem to appreciate the benefits.

Idea 32- Peer assessment and two stars and a wish

Occasionally it is effective to get pupils to assess each other's work. It encourages them to be reflective about their own. To make peer assessment effective I find that you need to give pupils examples of good assessment comments otherwise you may find they mostly feedback comments like 'nice pictures' and 'you could make your handwriting a bit neater', which don't help with learning a lot! Looking through one piece of work as a whole class and modeling some good feedback is a good technique for raising the quality of their peer assessment.

To ensure a balanced set of comments, both positive praise and areas for improvement, you may like to get your pupils to do ‘two stars and wish’. The idea is that each ‘star’ is a positive comment, praising some element of the work that has been done well and the ‘wish’ is a single comment explaining how the work could be improved.

Idea 33- Making corrections

Getting pupils to revisit marked work and make corrections is good practice. They cannot get away with the ‘I couldn’t do it so I didn’t bother’ attitude if they know you will chase up corrections. Whilst making corrections they are engaging with previous work and concepts which is important for long-term memory retention. Their work will also be correct throughout their exercise book which will be a good resource when it comes to revision time.

Idea 34- A sticky plenary

Feedback needs to be a two way process. You need to know what the pupils have learned as much as they need your feedback. That way you’ll respond to their learning needs better when you plan your next lesson. A nice plenary to get some instant feedback of what your pupils have learned is to give them all a sticky note, (some people might call them 'Post Its', but I don't want to be seen as endorsing one brand over another!) and give them some questions that you'd like them to answer on their sticky note. Once they've answered the questions they can stick the notes on your whiteboard. You can then either read them yourself to establish what the pupils have learned or even extend the plenary by having a class discussion about what you seen on the sticky notes. This is a nice plenary for getting participation going across the whole class and quality feedback from each pupil. I find you get out what you put in so choose your questions wisely!

Idea 35- Have a pen whilst you circulate

Marking is a time-consuming job that expands to whatever time you give to it. Whilst comments such as 'fantastic' and 'brilliant' certainly do have their place in keeping pupils' spirits and motivation up, quality marking also gives suggestions for improvement, corrections, and if necessary, worked examples.

Have a pen in your hand whilst you circulate around the room checking if pupils are on task and understanding the work. This is a nice tip that can significantly reduce the amount of time you spend marking. If you notice that a pupil has a certain misconception you can write in their book there and then, whilst in class, to point them in the right direction. Not only have you put them back on track quickly, you have also given them some quality written feedback in their book that you would otherwise have done when you were marking the books out of class. You are effectively using your circulation time to both check pupils' progress and also mark the books! There's not many 'two for the price of one' things in teaching so make the most of this one!

Idea 36- Mark backwards

How many times have you been marking a book and found that a pupil had a significant misconception that caused them to get everything wrong? You spend time doing worked examples and correcting some of their mistakes. Then you turn over the page to their workings from the next lesson when you see they then understood it fully and got them all right! What a waste of time all that feedback was because they did actually understand the topic after all!

One thing that can get around this problem is to mark backwards. That way, if you had two or more lessons on a topic you get to see the true extent of their understanding first and thus do not need to worry about correcting earlier lessons' work if they did understand in the end.

This isn't about being lazy and spending less time marking, it's about removing the unnecessary marking so you can give more time and effort to where it is most effective.

Idea 37- Get the learning conversation going in their books

Sometimes when you are marking books do you stumble across something that a pupil has got wrong but can't work out what their misconception is? Getting a regular learning conversation going in their books is a great way to get around this and many other problems. The idea is that pupils have to regularly comment about their understanding of the work. If they don't understand something they have to describe which bit exactly. Writing 'I don't get it' is off the table and they have to be more specific, like 'I understand how to find equivalent fractions but don't understand what a common denominator is'. Naturally you can then respond to their comment when you mark their books.

Getting a learning conversation going helps you be more effective with your marking and creates a good rapport with your pupils as you are responding to their learning needs directly rather than being generic. It also encourages pupils to be reflective and better problem solvers. Being able to explain which part of a concept they don't understand and thus knowing what they need to learn is going to be a very important skill in the skills-based, rather than knowledge-based economy of the future.

Idea 38- Good marking is about balance. Choose the right approach at the right time

You can't do thorough close marking, correcting every error and mistake in the books of every pupil you teach each week. No full time teacher has time to do that. It is also important that marking does not take over your home life. Since marking will expand to the time you give it, set your time allowance before you begin and stick to it, checking your progress regularly and adjusting the 'depth' of your marking to make sure you are going to hit your deadline.

If you can get pupils to mark their own or their peers' work in class as often as possible, you can focus your attention and time on the things they got wrong and correcting it rather than establishing what they got right or wrong in the first place. If you see a page full of ticks you know they understood the topic and a 'quick tick and flick' approach is appropriate. Take the time you have saved on this book and add it on to what you spend on another where the pupil got things wrong.

Finally, be realistic about how regularly and thoroughly you can mark your books. At different times in the year, different classes will become the priority. Give your priority class the majority of your marking time.

Idea 39- Get parents to sign off homeworks

Do the parents/guardians of your pupils discuss their child's homework with them? When setting and collecting homeworks consider establishing the rule that a homework is not complete until your parents/guardians have signed and dated it.

The benefits of this approach are to get parents engaging in the pupils' work with them and raising awareness of their child's progress. If the parent/guardian has regular sight of a child's exercise book, the more assertive ones will support you in advising the child how to improve. If they see your comments in the child's book they are more likely to reinforce the message and check that the child is following through on your suggestions in this weeks' homework.

Idea 40- The praise-criticism-praise sandwich

If you've got a criticism to deliver, whether it is in a book whilst marking, or in class you may like to consider using the *praise-criticism-praise sandwich* technique. As the name suggests, you deliver the criticism in between two positive comments. For example: "Well done on getting questions 1 to 3 right, Tom. I am disappointed that you did not attempt question 4. Making mistakes is part of learning and if you make the effort to have a go at each question then your learning will progress much faster" or "You have made good progress towards reaching your grade B, Mary. However, your behaviour in class is preventing you from reaching your potential. If you can make a positive change by applying yourself to your work in class fully from now on you should reach your grade B that you are capable of."

Somehow starting and ending positively helps the delivery of the critical comment be less personal and negative. There are certainly times when pupils need to just be told things straight as they are. At other times this technique is helpful.

~***~

Managing Behaviour

The need to know the capital of Florida died when my phone learned the answer. Rather, the students of tomorrow need to be able to think creatively: they will need to learn on their own, adapt to new challenges and innovate on-the-fly.

Anthony Chivetta

Idea 41- Consistency is key

The first piece of advice I was ever given about behaviour management was the best I have ever heard. Consistency is key. Set your rules and stick to them. Someone said to me once that kids actually like rules. They actually like the structure and the security and I agree with them. Speak to pupils and you'll find that they can't stand teachers who are inconsistent with their discipline and who have 'favourites'. The teachers they like the best are often the strictest. But I think the quality they warm to is the consistency.

Idea 42- Oak trees stand firm, but they do bend in the wind

Consistency is the backbone of discipline, but a backbone wouldn't be much use unless it can flex. Oak trees are strong monoliths but they do sway in the wind. There is certainly a time to move established boundaries and rules to accommodate the circumstances at hand. If it is a sweltering day and the school rule is that pupils must wear blazers at all times, would it be reasonable to allow them to take them off just for your lesson to make them more comfortable and thus help with the learning?

If you are going to relax or alter an established rule for a limited period of time I believe you do need to be assertive about it. Explain why you are doing it and the timeframe for this exception. Also beware of setting precedents and what the implications could be in the future.

I think Sue Cowley sums it up perfectly in her excellent book, *Getting the buggers to behave*: be reasonable, but don't reason.

Idea 43- The private chat

Teenagers often care deeply about their 'image' and what their peers think of them. It's sometimes a harsh social environment. Confronting a pupil in front of their peers can often lead to confrontation as they try to save their pride. It's a natural 'fight or flight' response where they decide to fight since fleeing is not an option.

If at all possible always reprimand a pupil privately. If this can't be done outside of the classroom then a quiet chat with them whilst the rest of the class is on task may be appropriate. You may decide that the best option is leaving the reprimand until the end of the lesson when you ask the pupil to remain behind for a discussion with you. Ultimately, your aim is to reprimand the pupil and explain to them why you are setting a punishment which is proportional to their misdemeanor. If you do it whilst they have the peer pressure to 'save face' you'll often find their reaction doesn't help achieve that aim.

Idea 44- You have two choices...

Imagine the scene. Tom is being disruptive. He keeps turning around for a chat with David who is sitting behind him. Other pupils see Tom doing this and are themselves beginning to get off task as they think you'll tolerate it. You have warned Tom and then you catch him at it again.

One technique I find very effective is to give pupils the 'option of the lesser of two evils'. For example, "Tom, I have asked you to not turn around and talk with David. You now have a choice. You can either move seats to sit on your own over there and continue with your work in silence or you can go stand outside in the corridor and we'll set you a detention at the end of the lesson". More often than not pupils will take the moving seats option. If you'd just asked them to move seats they would often protest and ask for another chance to remain where they are, but if you offer them this choice, for some reason they accept the 'escape route' option and do it. The pupil thinks they've got a mini-victory yet you've got exactly what you wanted!

Idea 45- Behaviour contract

If your school does not have an effective praise and reprimand system for behaviour, you may like to create your own. Making it a negotiated policy with the pupils is a good approach as it gets them thinking through the reasons behind it and what impact poor behaviour has on learning. They also have some ownership of the policy and feel more obliged to comply with it. Explain to them the importance of contracts in the real world and the great responsibility they have to put towards complying with them when they put their signature on the page. An agreed behaviour contract that is realistic and effective is vital for consistency, the backbone of discipline. It gives you an immovable anchor from which to refer back to in any incident. 'At the beginning of the year you signed our class behaviour contract where you agreed to...'

Idea 46- 'Please do this…' rather than 'Don't do that...'

Language can often be a subtle thing. The language you use can greatly affect the reaction you get from a pupil. 'Don't forget about the test marking deadline on Friday' or 'Please remember about the test marking deadline on Friday'. Which would you respond to better? The change in language is very subtle but what people could infer from the different approaches could be very different. The first option might suggest that you assume they will forget, whilst the second comes across more as a helpful reminder if they had forgotten.

Some teachers are quite thick skinned and may not respond that strongly to this nuance in the language, but pupils often do. 'Don't...' often comes across confrontational whilst 'Please do...' seems more respectful. Nonetheless, you can still say it in an authoritative tone that expects the instruction to be adhered to.

Another thing to look out for is starting a sentence with the word *why*. If often makes the sentence very personal. For example '*why* are you disrupting my lesson and preventing others from learning?' comes across with an overtone that there is something about you personally that I dislike, whereas '*what* is the reason that is preventing you from concentrating on your work and learning today?' makes it much more objective, less personal and more likely to get a positive response from the pupil.

Idea 47- A premature 'thank you'

Have you ever tried saying 'thank you' before a pupil has done something you asked them to? I know it sounds nonsensical but try it. Give a firm instruction then pause for half a second and say thank you still in a firm, expectant manner. The idea is that it creates a feeling of obligation on behalf of the student. If they have a conscience, they wouldn't want to not fulfill something that they've already received the (albeit tiny) reward of thanks for.

Idea 48- A broken record, a broken record, a broken record

Here's a secret weapon for those pupils who love to try to get you going off on a tangent whilst disciplining them. Think of a vinyl record that is perpetually skipping. Take on that role! Here's an example:

Teacher: Jade, I want you to pick up that piece of litter on the floor that I saw you drop.

Jade: It's not mine though, it's Dan's sweet packet, he threw it at me.

Teacher: Jade, I want you to pick up that piece of litter on the floor that I saw you drop.

Jade: Phoebe is nearer to it. Ask her to pick it up.

Teacher: Jade, I want you to pick up that piece of litter on the floor that I saw you drop.

Reluctantly, when she realises that she could be socialising with her friends rather than wasting her time in a confrontation that she can't win, Jade will often follow your instruction.

Idea 49- The power of silence

Are you comfortable with uncomfortable silences?! Most pupils are not! Use silence to your advantage. There are many times when holding a long silence sends a strong message of high confidence to the person you are speaking to.

Waiting in silence until you have everyone's attention in a class sends a powerful message of authority. It projects that you have high expectations. Do this repeatedly and the time you have to wait decreases as pupils realise your consistency.

Sometimes, the best thing you can do after asking a question is to keep silent for an extended period of time. If you've asked a pupil a question and they say 'I don't get it' clearly without thinking, just remain silent. They get uncomfortable and often then engage their thoughts and will offer an answer that they have then put some thought into. Often the best response to an 'I don't know' is no response.

Waiting in silence also sends the message that you are prepared to wait until you get the answer you want. In dealing with behavioural issues, for example when holding back a pupil over breaktime to discuss their poor behaviour with them, you may ask something like 'what do you think I am holding you insider for over breaktime to discuss?'. When the first 'I don't know' comes back at you just make strong eye contact, raise your eyebrow but remain silent. The pupil feels obliged to offer another answer. I have seen teachers do this to great effect and get the pupil to give a full blown account acknowledging their misdemeanor without the teacher saying a word. The body language is as important as the silence.

Finally, silence is a great way to stop a piece of poor behaviour escalating. A heated conversation can only escalate if both people allow it to. If one person wants to slow it down they can. If you have a pupil who answers back and tries to talk over you whilst you are explaining why you are disciplining them, try using long pauses in addition to the broken record technique. Begin you sentence over and over until they do not talk over you. The long pause is important as it slows them down and sends the message that the conversation is going to move at the pace you dictate. It is a powerful tool for sending a message of calm authority and control.

Idea 50- Parent power!

I often wonder if parents could see the way their child behaves at school, whether they would be surprised. School is a very sociable environment that brings out the personality in children whereas home life can more solitary.

Parenting is an incredibly difficult job, and many parents are happy for any support you can offer. Whenever a pupil is showing challenging behaviour in your lesson always consider ringing their parents for a discussion. Whilst not all parents are interested in their child's behaviour in school, I think it would be fair to say that the vast majority are. A discussion with a parent often leads to you learning some more context and useful information about the pupil and why they are misbehaving. Insist that schooling is a team effort and the parents can help you out by removing privileges at home should the child misbehave at school. I have found this to be a very effective strategy if the parents are supportive. The threat of removing their XBox is a strategy that seems to put the fear of judgment day into many pupils!

Many parents will get their child's version of events surrounding a behaviour incident and assume it is the whole truth. Making the phone call early, before the child gets home can help parents understand that there may be more to their child's behaviour issues at school than the child is telling them.

~***~

Motivation and Engagement

An education isn't how much you have committed to memory, or even how much you know. It's being able to differentiate between what you know and what you don't.

Anatole France

Idea 51- Give them choices and get them doing it for free

Once people feel comfortable and safe there are three factors that have been shown to be really important to their motivation level: **autonomy**, **mastery** and **purpose**. If you want to motivate pupils, or adults for that matter, strategies that focus on giving them a healthy blend of autonomy, mastery and purpose are a good way forward. Dan Pink is a well-known proponent of motivation strategies including these three factors and I'd strongly encourage you to check out his work.

Autonomy is all about giving people choices. Teachers are often used to the idea of offering pupils 'the lesser of two evils' as a strategy for dealing with poor behaviour. For example, 'you can move to the back of the room, sit quietly on your own and get on with your work or you can stand outside the classroom then do a lunchtime detention'. This embodies the idea of autonomy but does perhaps give it a somewhat negative spin!

Look at Wikipedia or the open-source software development communities online. Highly skilled, busy people are devoting hours of their time to developing high quality information content or software entirely for free. They could earn lots of money charging for their specialist skills yet they do it for nothing. Why? What motivates them to do this? I think it is a blend of autonomy and purpose. They can choose to work on the project if and when they like and they believe they are working towards a worthy achievement, something that money can't buy.

If you work as an engineer for Google you are allowed to spend Fridays working on whatever project you like. You can create your own project or work with peers you choose on other projects but ultimately you are not working on the project your boss has asked you to work on. Much innovation and many of Google's greatest products started life as these autonomous Friday projects. Autonomy makes people feel like they are in control of their own life which is a great motivator.

So how can you apply this to your classroom? How about offering a selection of activities pupils could choose to work on to learn a topic? How about doing one lesson per week or per fortnight when the pupils get to choose what they want you to teach them?

Have you tried setting voluntary homeworks? Don't laugh, try it! I personally have had success in getting pupils to do additional work towards their learning in my subject when I set them voluntary homeworks that are in addition to the minimum they must complete each week. These voluntary homeworks are often open-ended in nature which allows pupils to take them in whatever direction their personal interest and choices direct them and also distinguishes the homeworks from the more traditional '10 practice questions'.

Idea 52- Fun and healthy competition

Have you ever asked pupils what they think makes a good lesson? Without fail they nearly always say 'it was fun'. They don't seem to mention that lots of learning took place! Kids love to have fun and if we can wrap some learning into it then why not take advantage of the boost in your pupils' motivation by injecting some fun and healthy competition into your lessons?!

It's amazing what you can turn into a game... As a plenary last year I put together a simple set of questions that I wanted the pupils to answer. However, knowing that most of the class were obsessed with football, I decided to call it a 'penalty shootout' where two pupils in the class simply took it in turns to answer the questions. I had to calm them down in the end as they all wanted to have a go and asked for a penalty shootout in each lesson. If I'd have called it a 'topic summary' or a 'quiz' I'm sure they wouldn't have responded with such enthusiasm!

Idea 53- What's in it for me? Being contextual

If you are a believer in evolution then you'll think that we are not so different to our cave dwelling ancestors and thus many of our mental circuits will be programmed as theirs were. To them, obtaining a steady supply of food and water and reproducing to ensure the survival of the species took up most of their time. As their technology was fairly limited, many of their thoughts must have been occupied by fulfilling these primal needs. If you'd have tried to get a caveman to appreciate the beauty of a differential equation he'd probably have looked very bored. Show him a new way to catch a tiger and you'd have his full attention.

We pay attention to things that we think will benefit us. If we see no point in something, unless all our other wants and desires are satisfied, we are unlikely to invest time and attention into learning about it. In the history of the world we have never been confronted with as much information on a daily basis as what we get now and we all have to be selective over what we digest and what we ignore. Our interests and what we see as important in terms of our survival guide our choices.

Pupils won't pay attention to you long term just because you ask for it. They are not programmed that way. They will pay attention to contextual information that they see as interesting and useful to their lives. Make your lessons contextual and 'linked into their world' and getting their attention is a lot easier.

Idea 54- Life plans and taking the first step

Give pupils a purpose for studying hard in your subject. As well as making your lessons contextual and relevant to their lives, consider finding out about what they want to do with their lives and help them understand what they need to do to make it happen. As a tutor you could get pupils to write down where they want to go in life and all the steps that will get them there. Get them to put these up on the tutor noticeboard so they see something that is holding them accountable each day. Update them each year as their ambitions will undoubtedly change.

Have you ever not felt like going for a jog, but decided you really ought to, only to find that once you got out there you really enjoyed it? If they have a goal and the plan of steps to get them there, put a big emphasis on taking the first step. Getting off the start line is often a big mental barrier with many things in life so encourage them to make the first step a small one but to then definitely to take it. If they don't, ask them what the barrier to taking the first step is then do your best to remove it. Building momentum is important and getting going is the hardest part.

Idea 55- Praise the learning, not the getting things right

If you only praise the pupils who give the 'right' answers to questions you'll soon find that they are the only pupils who put their hands up. You get more of what you praise, so if we want the pupils to learn, praise the learning.

What does this look like in a classroom? In a plenary, rather than asking questions like 'How do I say "I have two sisters and a brother" in French?', ask 'What French have you learned today and how can you show me?'. If a pupil got a question wrong at the start of the lesson, ask them again at the end and praise the learning they have made. Encourage them to ask questions to further their knowledge. Put a poster above your board that says 'It's not the answers you give, but the questions you ask, that show me you are learning'.

Keep talking about learning rather than being right or wrong. Don't praise them for answering questions correctly at the start of the lesson if they walked in knowing the answer. Praise the ones who leave knowing more than they did when they walked in. Emphasise that making mistakes is a really important part of learning and if they aren't making mistakes we aren't pushing them far enough.

Idea 56- Stickers can move mountains

Unless they need a certain number to get their ticket for the school prom, you may find that merits mean little to pupils by the time they reach Year 11. However, give them a sticker and they'd jump through a flaming ring of fire for you! I have always found that investing the relatively small amount of money in some quality stickers is well worth it. Get stickers that are funny and quirky and you may find your pupils striving for one of these glittering medallions of adhesive wonder through increased quality in homeworks. Be tough and don't give out one your best stickers for just any piece of homework... Make them really work for it!

I really couldn't believe the effect on my pupils' motivation the first time I started using stickers. You'd have thought that it would be just the Year 7s who would go mad for them, but I have known 6ft tall Year 11 boys respond to them just as positively! You won't win them all over with a sticker but you'll be surprised what can be achieved!

Idea 57- Collaborative learning

Collaborative learning (working in groups) is a bit of a difficult strategy for me. I can understand that in some subjects it is desirable, or even necessary, yet in a maths classroom I have yet to see it used consistently effectively. I find pupils often see group work as an opportunity to let the 'best' student do the work while the others sit back and have a chat. No doubt I have things to learn myself about running a lesson based around collaborative learning, but I have heard similar feelings from other colleagues, even those with much more experience than myself.

Nonetheless, I can't convince myself to write off collaborative learning. I am totally convinced that if the practicalities and learning barriers mentioned above could be overcome, it would be a very powerful way for pupils to learn. There has been evidence to show it too. Dr Julie-Ann Edwards, a lecturer at The University of Southampton has looked into the benefits of collaborative learning in her research and found them to be significant. Feel free to do a search for Julie-Ann Edwards on the internet and read some of her papers. However, if you'd like to just know the headlines, listen to this anecdote that she told me whilst I was training to be a teacher:

Whilst working as a full-time maths teacher she decided to perform some research by using only collaborative learning styles for a whole school year with one class. At the end of the year the class outperformed the 'class above them' by a significant margin in the end of year exams.

There is a fine set of classroom management skills to be learned by us if collaborative learning is going to be this effective. A good publication I have personally consulted before is *Paired and group work for secondary school students in mathematics* by Roger Ray. This can be downloaded for free from http://www.eriding.net/maths/tl_resources_sec.shtml. Don't worry that it says it is for mathematics, many of the points would be relevant right across the subject spectrum. Have a read if you're interested in doing collaborative work in your classroom.

Idea 58- Put their progress up on the wall

It is much more motivating for a pupil to have a discussion about what progress they have made and how they can improve rather than just about what they are doing wrong. Putting their progress up on the wall, whatever format this takes is a very powerful motivation strategy.

In the past I have put module titles from the scheme of work up on the wall and ticked them off as we completed them. Another time I've allowed pupils to colour in learning objectives green on the wall next to their names when they have successfully met them. I think having something visual on the wall displaying progress helps build pupils' confidence. They reach certain 'key points' such as 'half way to level 5' and this seems to spur them on. It also seems to inject a dose of healthy competition between peers that some pupils respond really well to.

Idea 59- Put a smile on their face by putting one on yours

I was told on my teacher training course that the kids 'mirror your emotions'. It took me a while to truly accept this but the more I have reflected on my own experiences, the more I believe in it.

I have come to realise the power you have as teacher to change the mood of a class. Your relationships with a class can be viewed as a continuous spiral, but one that you can control if you can tame your emotions. If you have a bad lesson with a class and you go into their next lesson with frustration, you will certainly have a worse one. They respond to your body language and tone of voice and seem to get more difficult. The flip side is that this continuous self-reinforcing spiral can work the other way but only you can change the momentum. Being nicest to the class you like the least definitely yields benefits in terms of their behaviour, but it does take time. The inertia is slow. The more experienced teachers I have worked with say 'teaching is an act'. In this regard I do agree with them.

It's the hardest thing in the world to go from high frustration with one class, to greeting another with a smile on your face one minute later, but it's vital or you're making life even harder for yourself.

Idea 60- Get your tech on

I could write a whole book about how using ICT can increase pupil motivation and engagement (in addition to the learning benefits). Maybe I will one day! In the meantime there are many good books and internet blogs out there. A superb blog to have a read of if you are interested is *Edudemic* (http://edudemic.com/).

If you don't have a big technology budget, don't feel like you can't use ICT in your lessons. In recent years, computers have become nearer to being ubiquitous and there is a tidal shift at the moment towards mobile computing devices. It surprised me one day when I found out that every pupil in one of my Year 11 classes had an iPod Touch. If you are not familiar with these devices, they are like mini-computers which you can browse the Internet, send email, listen to music, watch videos and even word-process on. They are highly fashionable with the kids at present and I found that there were typically enough iPod Touchs in the room at any one time for atleast one-between-two with nearly every class. There are many free apps (computer programs) out there designed for learning purposes that pupils can be using in your lessons. I have had a lot of success with a free graph plotting app called QuickGraph, which is much better than the traditional graphic calculators.

It depends in what type of school and intake you have but you may find that pupils have mobile computing devices on them. If so you can creatively take advantage of this in your lessons. The kids often respond very enthusiastically with increased motivation. I met a headteacher once who showed me a textbook and said 'the kids won't read this, they say it's boring. But here's the exact same textbook on an iPod Touch and they love it'. Are the kids fickle? Maybe? Fight it or go with the tide? I'll let you decide!

~***~

Independent Learning

You cannot teach a man anything; you can only help him find it within himself.

Galileo Galilei

Idea 61- Ask the teacher as a last option

What do your pupils do if they're stuck? If the answer is ask you then you are going to be working very hard! Pupils I teach often ask me things like 'what's 3 times 6?'. Do you think I'd be doing them a favour by telling them the answer? They are broadcasting the message 'I can't be bothered to think and work it out for myself, you think for me'.

Make asking the teacher the last thing pupils do after they have exhausted all other options that they have available to them. This encourages independent learning habits and allows you to direct your time to where it is needed most. When your pupils are stuck get them into the habit of asking:

Myself- can I figure this out for myself?

My book- is there something in a textbook or one of my exercise books which can help me?

My nearby classmate- can the person sitting next to me help?

My teacher- ask the teacher for help

If you can get your pupils to work through this order of support when they are stuck, you cut out a very high proportion of the questions coming your way. The learning still happens and your pupils become better as independent learners. Bargain!

Idea 62- The solution isn't you working harder, it's them working harder!

Quite often, I think we beat ourselves up as teachers thinking about the 'kids who slipped through the net' and put the blame totally on our shoulders. We might think 'if only I'd have offered him some after-school tuition' or 'could I have provided some more differentiated resources to better meet their learning needs?'. Whilst this is very noble and certainly something we should reflect on, it would only have been effective if the child was willing to meet you half way by making the most of the extra time, support and effort you put in.

It worries me when teachers think that the solution to why a child is making no progress in their lessons rests solely on their shoulders and that if they only worked harder they'd make a difference.

Any increase in workload that you take on for a pupil needs to be at least matched by them. If they are not putting effort into completing their homework should you really be offering them extra tuition? What message is that sending to the child and the others in the class? I am a big fan of intervention when pupils are not making progress but ultimately the intervention should be designed to get the pupil working harder (if lack of effort is the issue) and not just something that makes work for the teacher. The focus is on what they need to do and you are there to facilitate the removal of barriers to learning and hold them accountable. Learning is a process that requires effort by both the teacher and the learner. I think we should always strive to remove all barriers to learning for pupils but they do have to take the initiative at some point themselves. They need to understand this. The more you spoon-feed them the more they'll let you. There's a saying about leading a horse to water...

Idea 63- Pupil plenaries

You don't know a topic until you can teach it. Let your pupils plan some lesson plenaries and you get numerous benefits including assessing how much they have learned, pupils consolidating their knowledge through teaching others and increased motivation as pupils have responsibility for the success of their lesson.

Planning forward by giving each pupil (or group) a specific learning objective to plan a plenary for encourages independent learning as they have to research the topic and become an 'expert' in that area in order to teach it to others. If they can't be bothered they let the whole class down and feel quite embarrassed by delivering such a poor learning experience which is in itself quite a good motivator for many pupils! Get the pupils who are more motivated to go first and this sets the bar high for others to aim at.

Idea 64- Magpie

We've all worked for bosses who love to steal your good ideas and claim them as their own. Why not encourage your pupils to be magpies? If they see a good idea in someone else's work they say 'magpie' and make a note of it in their book. As they accumulate great ideas in their book 'nest', they can periodically review them and try to incorporate them into their own work.

Idea 65- Independent learning graffiti wall

Showing pupils their progress on display is definitely a good thing. It motivates them and creates a healthy peer-pressure effect as pupils get competitive. Promote independent learning by covering one of the walls in your room with paper and get pupils to graffiti on the wall every time they do some independent learning explaining what they have done. Notice I said **graffiti** rather than **write**. What I mean is they can be a bit creative in their scribing which seems to inspire some pupils who are allowed to be 'naughty' in a controlled way but as a reward for doing good work! As the wall progresses, if it's done with multiple colours and images, it becomes visually appealing and encourages others to read it and use the writings in their own work. You can use the graffiti wall idea with other topics too rather than just independent learning.

Idea 66- Flip your classroom

There is fast-growing edu-philosophical movement called *The Flipped Classroom* that is causing shock waves through the educational community, particularly in America. I personally love the idea of the flipped classroom as it seems a more logical way to learn that the traditional model and technology has now reached a point where we can support the flipped model quite easily.

The idea is simply that rather than 'learning' at school and 'practising' at home, as in the traditional school model, pupils do the opposite. They typically watch online educational videos made by their teachers at home for homework where they learn new concepts. At school they do what they would have traditionally done for homework, practice questions and activities which gets them applying their knowledge. Classes typically involve lots of pair and group work to solve problems and promote learners sharing their knowledge with each other to find the solutions. The benefits of the flipped classroom are numerous and many teachers who have 'done the flip' now say they would never go back.

In the traditional classroom we typically expect pupils to learn new topics whilst they are in an environment full of distractions to their concentration. We then expect them to go home and complete exercises that get them to apply their knowledge. If they get stuck they are on their own with little or no support. In the flipped model pupils learn in a quiet environment where there are no or fewer distractions then they do the difficult part of applying their knowledge in class where they have many support options including their peers and the teacher.

In a traditional lesson you pace the delivery of the content towards the 'middle attainer' in the class and so some are struggling to keep up and the others are bored. In the flipped model pupils can truly work at their own pace with their learning.

Proponents of the flipped classroom model say pupils are much more motivated to learn as their learning becomes their responsibility and they enjoy the collaborative nature of the practice lessons.

The key that has unlocked the door of the flipped classroom model is the advance of technology. Creating videos and making them available online for your pupils is now a straight forward and free thing to do.

However, videos don't replace teachers. The role is just slightly different. You are more of a facilitator rather than a content deliverer. A video can't respond to questions from pupils and doesn't know how to explain a concept in different ways which a good teacher does. Nonetheless, if you free your hands of a lot of the content delivery, you can focus more on targeting your attention where it is needed which is correcting misconceptions with specific pupils.

Idea 67- Questioning and wait time

Most teachers apparently leave on average less than three seconds for students to think before accepting answers to questions. We often follow this up almost immediately with another question.

What kind of questions can be answered in three seconds?

Which of these is a question requiring only three seconds of processing time:

1. What is capital city of Brazil?

2. Why do you think some people have the view that using biofuels in our cars is not a good environmental solution?

One requires just basic recall, you know it or you don't, the other requires more thought and consideration of the question from different angles.

Don't fall into the trap of playing 'can you guess what is in my mind?' when you are using questioning in your classroom. If all you are doing is giving three second pauses and asking basic recall of knowledge questions then you might as well not be using questioning at all from an engagement perspective. Simply explaining would have a similar effect. Get your learners into the habit of knowing that when you ask them a question that you are expecting them to have to really think about the answer. Do this by choosing the wording of your questions wisely and allowing plenty of wait time. Getting pupils to think for some time individually then discuss and share their ideas with their partner is also a good tactic.

Aiming for questions that require thinking processes at the top levels of Bloom's Taxonomy (see idea 2) is a good idea. If pupils associate questions with having to think things through it promotes and develops their independent learning skills.

Idea 68- Edward De Bono's Six Thinking Hats

How can you teach how to think? We take for granted our ability as adults to think about things from different perspectives and evaluate ideas looking at both the pros and cons. Whilst many of us in our generation learned these skills in our adult lives through observing others, there are techniques to 'get them started early' these days that are genuinely useful. One such method is *Edward De Bono's Six Thinking Hats*.

The idea is that there are six different coloured 'thinking hats' that we put on at different times to ensure we fully think through an issue. Each coloured hat has a different 'thinking perspective'. The hats are:

White hat- associated with factual information. What do we know about this problem and what do we need to find out?

Yellow hat- associated with positivity and optimism. What are the positives and value in this option?

Black hat- associated with caution. What could go wrong? What are the disadvantages?

Red hat- associated with gut feeling and emotion. What does my intuition tell me about this problem? What is my emotional reaction to this?

Green hat- associated with creativity. What are some different options for solving this problem? What ideas have I got, no matter how crazy?

Blue hat- associated with logic. Now I have looked at all the different angles, what is the final decision?

If you want pupils to think in depth about a problem or issue from different angles you can say 'give me some yellow hat ideas about....' and then 'now give me some black hat about it'. The thinking hats provide a structured way of approaching thinking about issues or problems that ensures an adequate amount of time is given to each perspective. Pupils seem to engage with the hats and learn their meanings very quickly.

Why stop with the pupils? Have you ever been in a meeting where one person repeatedly finds fault with everything? Running meetings with specified times for considering ideas from each hat's perspective can be brilliant. Forcing people to be constrained to thinking only about the positives in an idea can balance out the natural negativity that can pervade some meetings. Giving a time limit to each hat allows people to give their black hat thoughts but restricts it to an appropriate amount of time. Also, starting off with 'give me some red hat about this idea' can be a great way of letting people get worries off their chest before you start to look at things objectively.

Idea 69- Results-Only Learning Environment (ROLE)

To promote the value of independent thinking and encourage more of it, many teachers, particularly in the USA, are adopting a *Results-Only Learning Environment*

(ROLE). The idea is that you set pupils projects and challenges and assess them only on the results and mastery of the learning outcomes, not the method used to get them.

ROLE is a whole philosophy of teaching that goes wider than just how we facilitate learning. It promotes student autonomy and does not allow traditional worksheets, homeworks and direct instruction. Grading and percentage scores are dismissed with, to be replaced with comment-only marking giving narrative feedback. There are certainly links between a ROLE and a Flipped classroom model. It blends in some problem solving and enquiry based learning methods to. It's a whole learning culture. Why not give it a go? There is plenty of useful information about how to implement a ROLE at the end of a Google search if you are interested.

Idea 70- The importance of planning and deadlines in independent learning

From a teacher's point of view, pure independent learning would be a nirvana. Imagine a classroom where every pupil could be working on their own topic and had the initiative to choose which questions and activities to work on. They would reflect on their results and plan what topics they needed to revisit and they would remain motivated and on task with their learning. In this blissful place your pupils' first response when they are challenged by a question wouldn't be 'I don't get it', but rather 'I'll go and speak to Tom about it and get him to teach me because I know he understands this'. This doesn't mean you wouldn't have a job to do. You would monitor pupils' progress and help out the ones who really needed it with some quality one-to-one time.

Whilst we dream of teaching in this serene paradise, the truth is that it is something to aspire to as our pupils do not have the independent learning skills to manage their learning in this way. This is not a dig at them at all; more a consequence of the way we have taught for hundreds of years with the teacher being the funnel through which all knowledge can be passed on.

So in the real world, if you are getting your pupils to do some independent learning you will need some strategies to support them as they make the transition from being passive listeners to active learners.

Pupils seem to have a natural desire, at least at first, to want to study things they can already do. Many have some barriers, often emotional self-confidence issues that mean that they stay within their safe zone, relearning what they already know and not challenging themselves. Whilst I wouldn't use the technical language, I think it is worthwhile to talk to pupils about Piaget's *Zone of Proximal Development*, the theoretical space of things pupils can learn with some support. Explaining how learning only happens when they make mistakes and push themselves outside of their comfort zones is very important. Your role is to monitor this and ensure that they are adequately challenging themselves. Make them accountable to you and possibly even get them to write an 'independent learning plan' where they explain to you what they are going to do and get your approval before they do it. Then get them to report on what they have learned at the end of carrying out the plan. Your role is one of monitoring, guidance and direction. You may like to regularly meet with each pupil for a '3 minute progress check' in lessons that ensures they are challenging themselves and also keeping the pace of their learning at a rate that is appropriate for them.

Independent learning is something that I believe very passionately in. If you want to learn anything in the real world once you leave school you almost certainly will have to do it yourself. Teaching our pupils independent learning skills is incredibly important as they will have them for life. I don't feel as though I have anywhere near mastered this in my own classes yet as it is a real challenge when pupils are so used to being passive listeners and never having to take some initiative for themselves. Nonetheless, let's not give up! Let's try to support them on their journey towards becoming independent learners by ensuring they plan their learning to be challenging and also have someone to be accountable to.

~***~

'High Ability' Students

I have come to the frightening conclusion that I am the decisive element. It is my personal approach that creates the climate. It is my daily mood that makes the weather. I possess tremendous power to make life miserable or joyous. I can be a tool of torture or an instrument of inspiration, I can humiliate or humor, hurt or heal. In all situations, it is my response that decides whether a crisis is escalated or de-escalated, and a person is humanized or de-humanized. If we treat people as they are, we make them worse. If we treat people as they ought to be, we help them become what they are capable of becoming.

Johann Wolfgang von Goethe

This section is about things awesome teachers do with students that have a high ability in their subject. There are many names given to these pupils, 'able', 'gifted', 'talented', 'gifted and talented' and so on. I settled for 'high ability' for the chapter title as I think it needs little explanation! The focus of this section is in strategies that help you make sure you are challenging and sufficiently stretching the learning of these pupils in class. Please don't think these strategies are only for use with high ability pupils. Whilst they are particularly suitable with the high fliers, many of them are good for use right across the whole ability spectrum.

Idea 71- Teaching others isn't a cop out and mentoring others is good too

What do you do when one of your pupils completes all the work you ask of them in class? I remember many of my own teachers at school asking that person to 'be another teacher' and circulate around the room, helping other pupils who needed it. For some reason, when I started teaching myself, I was given the impression that this was somehow a cop out strategy that lazy teachers used if they hadn't prepared some extension material. I personally strongly disagree with this view.

Asking pupils to explain concepts to other pupils and help them with their understanding is a valuable exercise. There is a difference between knowledge and understanding and being able to teach a topic is that difference. You may be able to apply a new skill learned but to be able to teach it you need to be able to break it down into a logical structure with increasing layers of complexity that you can explain to someone else. To be able to teach a topic you need to be able to understand the limitations and exceptions of the concepts. Asking pupils with mastery of a topic to assist pupils still struggling with it definitely benefits both of them.

No matter how many times you remind pupils of your 'open door' policy where they can come and see you any breaktime, lunchtime or after school for some help with their homework, few do. However, if you get high attaining kids from older year groups to mentor struggling younger pupils many do seem to respond and meet regularly with their mentor for some extra tuition. Once again the mentoring arrangement is beneficial to both students.

Idea 72- What if...

Have you ever tried to teach the probability scale to high ability pupils? I assure you it can be one of the most frustrating and stressful experiences of your life! The idea is you ask pupils to make up statements and place the probability of them happening on a number line that runs from zero (impossible) up to one (certain). Once you've got past the misconception that the probability of it raining today is not '0.5 because it either rains or it doesn't', you then ask for statements that have a probability of either one or zero of happening. A pupil might say something like 'the probability that the Earth will end tomorrow is zero'. Another pupil will immediately interject that the probability of this happening is close to zero, but not zero as there could be a huge inbound asteroid that we don't know about yet. A pupil might say 'the probability that tomorrow will be Tuesday is one'. Another will immediately reply 'no, that's not true, it's very close to one but what if the government decides today to change the names of the days. It's been done before...'. Before the disagreements get out of hand you emphasise how difficult it is to think of things which truly have a probability of one or zero of happening but it's great that they get the idea.

Rather than complaining about how the kids 'find holes in everything' we should applaud their nature. One thing that makes them such good learners is that they constantly question things and push the boundaries of ideas and concepts. They test ideas to destruction and find their limitations. The more 'what if' questions you get from pupils, the more they are learning. It's often frustrating to be on the receiving end but do encourage your pupils to ask 'what if' questions as they really support learning.

Idea 73- Show me that you understand...

Giving people the opportunity to be creative is often a fantastic motivator. Consider now and again offering your high ability pupils the opportunity of choosing their own homework to demonstrate to you that they understand a topic. If they want to answer ten questions off a worksheet then that's fine but if they want to make a poster or a presentation then that's also great too. Perhaps they might like to make an audio podcast or a video tutorial. At the end of the day, does it really matter what format a piece of work is in if they show understanding? Empower your pupils with 'choose a way to show me you understand' homework!

Idea 74- Aim for the upper levels of Bloom's Taxonomy

If you subscribe to the idea of Bloom's Taxonomy (see earlier in the book) then you really should be providing your high ability pupils with tasks and activities that meet the higher tiers of the Taxonomy: analysing, evaluating and creating.

This may sound silly, but as I'm not a teacher whose students are assessed on their language writing and critiquing abilities, I often forget the subtle differences between analysing and evaluating. I understand how creating is different, but, if you share my difficulty, the difference between analysing and evaluating is the following:

Analysing: the task of separating an idea or a concept into its component parts so the organisational structure can be understood. The purpose is typically for explanation or interpretation.

Evaluating: the task of making judgements about the value of ideas or concepts.

What tasks you give your pupils will of course be subject specific, but I find a general reminder to myself every now and then to keep giving analysing, evaluating and creating based tasks to my high ability pupils helpful, as it prevents me falling into the trap of only giving knowledge-recall and applying-knowledge based tasks.

Idea 75- To enrich, extend or accelerate? That is the question

How you challenge your high ability pupils can take different forms and I think it is very important to remember this. With the pressure of certain statistical measures which are meant to assess the performance of a school relying on pupils getting more and more qualifications, it is perhaps not surprising that many schools just accelerate their high ability pupils. Another GCSE is worth a lot of 'value added points' to the school etc.

However, if you have the luxury of not playing to the tune of the statistics, consider taking advantage of enrichment or extension approaches for your high ability pupils. Pupils often complain that they see no point in many things they learn as they won't use them in later life. An enrichment task that challenges them to apply their learning in a real world context can do wonders for pupils' motivation and gives their learning greater meaning.

In a nutshell: don't just give them the tools, give them something to fix by using them now and again.

Idea 76- Four ways to differentiate

Did you know there are at least four ways to differentiate learning? Consider challenging your pupils by differentiating:

By task: Get your high ability pupils on a different task to the rest of the class. Put quite simply, give them more challenging work to do!

By resource: Whist they are doing the same task as the rest of the class, give high ability pupils a different resource. This could be a more in depth text with more technical language for example.

By outcome: Expect your high ability pupils to complete more of the work than the rest of the class. If you are asking pupils to complete ten questions, tell your high ability pupils you expect them to complete fifteen.

By support: If your high ability pupils are reasonable independent learners challenge them to teach themselves a topic with less support from yourself. Act as a 'mentor', checking up on their progress and directing them where to go next rather than just being a deliverer of information. If you can cut the chord somewhat with high ability pupils without reducing their learning then definitely do so as it is good for their development as independent learners.

Idea 77- Problem solving and enquiry based learning

Pupils often get talked at by teachers and expected to sit, listen and digest what is being presented to them. The result, after day-in-day-out of this approach is that they become very passive learners. The information goes in through the eyes and ears but does not necessarily engage the brain in the process.

In my pre-university days I lived with someone who was studying retail management. They attended university for five days each week for three years learning how to run a shop. At no point in their course did they spend time in shops seeing what the practicalities of the job were. How can you learn how to run a shop without experiencing it for real? I believe often 'learning on the job' is the best way to learn as you very quickly find out what the important things to learn are and what things you can ignore. People say you learn to pass your driving test, then you learn to drive, and they're right!

Why not take the same approach sometimes with your pupils? Start a topic with a problem to be solved. This way pupils cannot be passive. They have to think and try to apply some knowledge. It's wonderful to watch pupils' intuition guide them and see them approach a problem in different ways. Once they see there is a problem to solve, they often then see a reason for learning something new and will be more motivated to learn it. A superb teacher who passionately believes in a problem-solving approach to learning is Dan Meyer who writes his blog *dy/dan* (http://blog.mrmeyer.com/). I thoroughly recommend it as a good read if you are interested.

Another approach to ensure your pupils are actively, rather than passively learning is to use enquiry-based learning. Developed in the 1960s, this approach assumes a *constructivist* style of learning where pupils 'form their own knowledge' through investigating concepts. For example, rather than telling pupils that 'two minus signs make a plus', you might instead get them filling in multiplication tables including negative numbers following the number patterns and then get them to 'create' the two minus signs rule by themselves by looking at the results.

Idea 78- Read deep

Do your pupils just read up on a topic on Wikipedia and assume then that they know everything there is to know about it? The world treats knowledge these days as though it is fast food; easy to find and consume. I call it a *fast knowledge* culture. Why bother spending time going to the shop, buying a newspaper and reading the opinion pages when you can get a short, 'bitesize' fact based news article online? Who has time for anything deeper than that? Well, we all should in my opinion as this fast knowledge culture is ruining our pupils' ability to study things in depth and to 'read around' a topic to understand it from different people's perspectives. Furthermore, we now have a generation of pupils who have grown up with fast knowledge and never known anything different. If you grew up only eating fast food, you would never know the health benefits of eating fresh fruit and vegetables. Your physical development would be restricted. If you grow up only with fast knowledge, how will you ever appreciate the complexity and detail of the big issues in the world and appreciate the differing viewpoints of people around you? Your intellectual development will be restricted.

Don't let your pupils only consume fast knowledge! Encourage them to read deeply on a topic. That means if they have read a book about something, get them to read another on the same topic and compare the similarities and differences. Having the occasional 'you're not allowed to read about this on the internet' day is good for pupils too.

Idea 79- Play devil's advocate

Being able to back up your thoughts with evidence and reason is a very important life skill that pupils should be exposed to. If a pupil expresses an opinion or a thought in response to a question you have asked, play devil's advocate and challenge it, getting them to justify their response. For example:

Pupil: I think we should abandon capitalism.

Teacher: Why?

Pupil: Because there are lots of poor people in the world and the gap between the rich and the poor keeps getting bigger?

Teacher: Ok, that sounds like a good idea. What would you do instead?

Pupil: Oh, um. I don't know.

Teacher: Well we can only leave it behind if you have something better in mind.

Pupil: What about communism?

Teacher: Has that been successful in the past? What makes you think it would be successful in today's world?

Playing devil's advocate, trying to pick holes in pupils' reasoning, if done in a way that is sensitive and doesn't try to humiliate them, encourages them to think deeper about questions and issues as well as giving them the very important life skill of thinking things through thoroughly.

Idea 80- Formal debating

Why not set up a formal debate in your classroom? Emphasise the civilised etiquette that is required in such an event and allow pupils plenty of time to prepare their arguments. After each side has presented their for or against argument get a moderator to take questions from the audience. Ask the panels to challenge the other side's arguments too. After a final closing argument from each side get the audience to vote on whether they are for or against the motion.

I am personally a big fan of formal debating as it teaches pupils many skills such as how to discuss disagreements in a civilised manner, how to logically support an opinion with evidence, presentation skills and that there are issues in the world that don't have straightforward answers.

~***~

Special Educational Needs

Do not confine your children to your own learning, for they were born in another time.

Chinese Proverb

Giving all children with learning difficulties the 'Special Educational Needs' label isn't exactly helpful in appreciating the diversity of pupils' needs out there. Indeed even giving children the dyslexia or discalculia label could over simplify things since many of the learning difficulties are based on a spectrum. Every child is different and that's true of their learning difficulties and needs. The ideas discussed here should not be seen as 'solutions' to helping all children with SEN but rather some strategies that you might like to employ if the specific learners in front of you could benefit from them. There is of course not a one-size-fits-all solution, rather a variety of strategies that a good teacher knows when to use for specific pupils. I thought long and hard about whether to include this section on SEN in the book. I am very conscious about not wanting to be seen to deskill the complex and professional work that specialist teachers do in this area by presenting it as crude 'top ten tips'. In contrast, it is my intention to raise awareness of the need for every teacher to learn about specific strategies for meeting the learning needs of all pupils in their class, including the ones with SEN. I hope you see this section as 'food for thought' rather than 'a list of everything I need to know'.

Idea 81- Make the most of your SENCO

My teacher training did not, in my opinion, prepare me adequately for meeting the learning needs of SEN pupils in my classes. Nearly everything I have learned about teaching strategies for SEN pupils was learned in the job. Your school will have a Special Educational Needs Coordinator, SENCO, who should be a valuable resource for learning how to best cater for these pupils. I have always found SENCOs to be very willing to meet, discuss and share ideas. I guess in part it must be because we are taking an interest in the important work they do and asking out of curiosity rather than because it is compulsory. Each time I have met with a SENCO I've come away with a tangible strategy to use in my classes and happy to have learned something new. Definitely use your SENCO. They are so important.

Idea 82- One instruction at a time and break tasks down into steps

Saying 'Unpack your bags, get out your books, write the title Evaporation, write the date then have a think about how you think the water that falls as rain gets up into the sky in the first place' is not going to be helpful for some SEN pupils. None of these tasks are particularly challenging, but if all delivered at once, they may not be completely followed. Be conscious and wary of wrapping lots of mini-tasks up into a big one such as this. Deliver one instruction at a time and wait until it has been achieved before moving on. If there is a challenging single task, such as write a story set in medieval England, break it down into a series of smaller mini-tasks.

Idea 83- Worked examples and 'what you're aiming for' pieces of work

Many SEN pupils respond well to being shown a piece of work that models what you want them to achieve. For example, rather than saying ‘line up your equals signs’ and ‘make sure you present each piece of your workings on a new line’, they seem to respond better to being shown a well presented piece of work. As they say on Blue Peter... *Here’s one I made earlier!*

Idea 84- Key info sheets

I have heard many names for these but the idea is that you give pupils a ‘key info’ sheet of paper to support them as they are working. This could contain important vocabulary, formulas, facts, definitions, diagrams or whatever is appropriate for your subject. It is important that they have them every lesson so they ‘learn’ what is on the sheet and instinctively know there is something on the there to help them with the current question at hand. Get them laminated and they’ll last you a long time. Have a good search on the internet to find one rather than making one as there are many freely available for download.

Idea 85- Routines

Many SEN pupils, particularly those on the autistic spectrum, do not respond well to change. Creating set routines provides familiarity and consistency that many SEN pupils respond well to. This could take many forms such as the way you like them to enter the room and begin a lesson, regularity in the days of setting and collecting homework or the way you like them to present their work and the routines you create to support this.

Idea 86- Copying off the board isn't good

I was told once that some SEN pupils find the process of copying off the board very difficult. The repetitive looking up and down is difficult for them as it takes them time to relocate where they have got up to on the board. I'm not sure if there is academic research to support this but from personal experience I think it is sound advice.

There are several things you can do to improve this situation. If you can give them a textbook or worksheet containing the information then do it. I have seen teachers print off their slides onto worksheets and remove some words from them so that the pupils have most of the copying down done for them, but they have to fill in just a few gaps to keep them engaged. Another suggestion if you do have to use the interactive whiteboard is to alternate highlighting each line of text with a different colour, e.g. blue, yellow, blue, yellow... This apparently makes it much easier for them to find where they have got up to.

Idea 87- Coloured background to board and worksheets

Many pupils, particularly some with dyslexia can read faster if the paper from which they read off is coloured rather than white. Yellow or blue seem to be the most popular colours in my experience but it is important to know which colours each pupil prefers because one that reads faster with a blue background will probably not be as fast with a yellow background. Speak to your SENCO to find out the needs and preferred colour background of pupils in your class. If you are using an interactive whiteboard you can quite often tint the background of the screen to whatever colour is required.

Idea 88- Think carefully about the seating arrangement

Give considerable thought to the seating arrangement and where you place your SEN pupils in your classroom.

Naturally, if pupils have reading difficulties or visual impairments, put them closer to the board. If they have hearing difficulties make sure they are seated at the front nearest to where you teach from. If a pupil has ADHD, consider seating them in a position so as to reduce the number of distractions. I have found that sometimes autistic pupils have a particularly close friend and they will work much better with them beside them rather than anyone else. Get into the habit of consciously regularly checking that the seating arrangement isn't acting as an obstacle to the learning of your pupils.

Idea 89- 'Get a wiggle on' is not a good thing to say

Some pupils with SEN, particularly those on the autistic spectrum can interpret things that you say very literally. They often don't get the meaning of metaphors or sarcasm so make sure you avoid these. Phrases such as 'get a wiggle on', 'move it', 'put your foot down', 'we haven't got all day', 'knuckle down' and 'press on' should be avoided. Concentrate on giving clear, unambiguous instructions that can be taken literally.

Idea 90- Comic Sans size 14

Similar to the idea about using a coloured background, the reading speed of some SEN pupils can be affected by the size and the font of what they are reading. Check with your SENCO about the specific preferences of the pupils in your class. This would be better than assuming they all prefer one particular font and size. Although, I do know of a head teacher who made all their staff produce their worksheets in Comic Sans, size 14 font! I'm not sure of the basis of this decision but they were very insistent that Comic Sans was a font that dyslexic pupils found relatively easy to read. I wouldn't be so broad brush if I were you! Check the needs of your individual pupils with your SENCO.

~***~

Making the Learning Stick

I have never let my schooling interfere with my education.

Mark Twain

Idea 91- Relearning- The Ebbinghaus Forgetting Curve

Why do our pupils seem to forget most of what they learn from one day to the next? It's because they are human beings and we all do! It's all to do with the *exponential nature of forgetting* and it's something every teacher needs to be aware of and plan for.

In 1885 Hermann Ebbinghaus, a German psychologist published his hypothesis, *Über das Gedächtnis* (Memory: A Contribution to Experimental Psychology) which built its ideas off the hypothesis of the exponential nature of forgetting. Before I dive into the detail here it is worth saying that Ebbinghaus conducted his experiments which support his hypothesis on himself so his ideas could be accused of lacking scientific rigour. Nonetheless, through experience both in the classroom and thinking about my own learning I believe his idea of a *Forgetting Curve* to be useful and accurate enough to have a tremendous impact in our classrooms and the way our pupils learn.

The idea can be explained like this: think of our brains as being like a sieve. Knowledge is constantly seeping out through the holes in the sieve. If a sieve is full of water it drains out quickly, but as time goes on, as the water level drops the speed at which water is leaving the sieve slows down. Memory works the same way too. When you learn something new you start forgetting it very quickly! As time goes on the speed you are forgetting something slows down, but of course by then you have forgotten most of it!

This looks pretty dire! How many times have you heard teachers saying 'they couldn't remember a thing and they only learned it yesterday!'. We shouldn't be surprised as we all work the same way. Nobody remembers something for the long term if they 'learn' it once and never think about it again. Ebbinghaus suggested that there are a number of factors that affect how fast we forget things, how steep the graph is, which include the difficulty of the learned material, stress and sleep. Nonetheless, we all follow the same general trend of forgetting things exponentially over time.

Fortunately there is hope! If we want to commit something to long term memory we can, quite easily. It's all about three things: repetition, repetition, repetition. Going back to the sieve analogy, think of the sieve as being 'filled with learning water' once and then when it is half drained we fill it again. Here's the magic. As we fill it a second time the holes in the sieve get smaller meaning that the level of water falls slower. Fill it up again and the holes get smaller still. By repeating our learning about a topic the speed at which you forget it slows down. There is no more powerful argument for revision than the Ebbinghaus Forgetting Curve.

The impact of understanding the ideas behind the Forgetting Curve should have profound effects on our practice as teachers. However you do it, you need to schedule in some time for relearning. This could take many forms and no doubt you are already doing it but here are some ideas of things you could do:

1. Starters where pupils have to explain what they learned in your lesson yesterday, last week and last month.

2. Starters where you do quick tests on topic that have been covered before.

3. If you can get the whole-school onboard, starters where you ask what they learned in their previous lesson.

4. End of unit assessments to revise for.

5. Opportunities to reread through notebooks and exercise books.

6. Good old-fashioned homework set on topics that you covered a while ago

Something I find particularly interesting about the ideas behind the Forgetting Curve comes to the surface when pupils or colleagues try to show its principles are not universal by giving the names of people who learn things once and remember them forever. We all enjoy teaching the kids who you just have to explain things to once, but questioning I have done with these types of pupil, suggests something very powerful about the Forgetting Curve. The 'tell them once and they remember it forever' kids are relearning things. They do it simply by thinking through the topic at regular intervals afterwards, making connections to other things they know and trying to think about how they can apply the knowledge to their lives. The big message is that you don't have to be in a classroom to relearn something. Simply taking some time to think something through again is enough. I personally believe this sheds light on why 'being interested' is so important when it comes to learning. You wouldn't rethink through something that you weren't interested in. If we make our subjects interesting and engaging I do believe that a lot of the relearning that is so important to long term memory retention would be done automatically by the kids' curiosity rather than by our prescribed activities and homeworks.

Idea 92- Consolidation lessons aren't a bad thing

I got caught out during a formal lesson observation once. We had just finished a series of lessons about solving quadratic equations and I thought I'd round off the topic with a consolidation lesson based around a lovely jigsaw activity. The puzzle featured quadratic equations that needed matching up with their solutions. In addition to this, there were key facts to remember which were put into sentences and split up between pieces that needed matching up. It was a large puzzle so I split the class into four groups of five pupils to encourage some team work and promote discussion about the topic between pupils. The lesson went fantastically well with many an interesting discussion had and many a misconception dispelled. Pupils left the room with a better understanding of how to solve quadratic equations than when they came in and they were much faster and more accurate at solving them.

Grading for that lesson: satisfactory

Since I hadn't 'shown any new learning' in my pupils in this lesson it was graded satisfactory! Whilst I was naturally disappointed with this result I quickly moved on and learned my own lesson about the requirements of a 'formal observation'. Again, what you do for that and what you should be doing day-to-day are different.

Consolidation lessons are very important. I would, and still do, run the quadratic equations lesson again when it is appropriate for pupils to consolidate their learning on that topic. I could be sucked into discussing at length about my feelings about why a 'formal observation' should only look at one particular type of lesson where 'new learning' is shown but I shall refrain. I think it is more important to say that on a day-to-day basis getting the correct balance between new learning and relearning is the most important thing. Don't view 'new learning' lessons as being the only good ones. You can still deliver a brilliant or awful consolidation lesson too.

You can look at consolidation lessons in terms of the Forgetting Curve and they fit nicely for promoting the relearning part of the curve. However, an interesting alternative perspective about the process of consolidating learning comes when you think of it in terms of your conscious and subconscious brain. Practice does not make perfect, practice makes permanent. When we learn new things we have our conscious brain fully engaged to the task, but as we relearn and practice that task the processing moves over from our conscious to our subconscious brain. Do you have to think consciously about how to walk, talk, drive, read or anything else that you repeatedly do on a daily basis? You can achieve similar levels of 'automation' with any task if you practice enough. Consolidation is vital. I speak from a maths perspective but I'm sure it will be applicable in other subjects. You cannot teach pupils how to factorise numbers until they 'know' their times tables. When you try to teach this lesson you find that their conscious brain is fully occupied trying to calculate their times tables that little processing is left over for learning the concept of factorisation.

You can't run until you can walk subconsciously and it is the same in many areas of knowledge.

Consolidation must be done and learners must understand why practising something they can 'already do' is so important.

Please take the time to read *Incognito: The Secret Lives of The Brain* by David Eagleman. This book is a captivating read for anybody involved in working with brains, like us teachers are! It presents fascinating insights into the weird and wonderful way our brains work including such things as how our subconscious brain can learn something without our conscious brain being aware of it, why you notice when your name is mentioned in a conversation that you didn't think you were listening to, and why it is possible to get angry with yourself. The revelations have big implications for many areas of society including dating, drug use, criminal law, artificial intelligence and infidelity. It was this book that made me realise how important consolidation lessons are and I highly recommend it to you.

Idea 93- It's been emotional

Where were you when JFK was assassinated? What were you doing on 11th September 2001? What was your first day at school like?

Having a strong emotional response to an event can certainly put the experience into long term memory. I can remember only a handful of lessons from my schooling but they all share the theme of generating a strong emotional reaction. Some were positive emotions and others not so positive. Ask me the emotion I was feeling for each of the experiences I can remember from my school days and you'd have the complete spectrum by the time I'd finished. It doesn't matter which emotion we associate with an experience, if it is sufficiently strong enough we'll remember it. The best and most memorable stories are the ones where you are going through the emotional rollercoaster alongside the characters.

You can't make every lesson induce amazement and wonder in your pupils, but the more you do, the more they'll take away with them for the rest of their lives. Use humour, stories, kindness and any other emotive tools you have to stimulate great learning in your classroom.

Idea 94- Let them revise in their preferred learning style

Encourage students to experiment with different ways of revising to see what seems to work for them. I personally wouldn't make too much of a fuss about telling pupils about learning styles. We can all learn in all styles, but we do have preferences. I would discourage you from labeling students as 'visual learners' etc because it can give them an excuse to switch off when they are not getting a visual input from you. Instead, taking the approach of getting them to try out different approaches and be conscious of what works for them encourages more independence in their learning and self-awareness.

Idea 95- Follow me cards with a whole class

Create a class set of domino cards with the purpose of summarising all the key points on a topic. On the first domino write ‘START’ on one half then start a sentence on the other, e.g. ‘Henry VIII had...”. On the next domino you put the second half of the first sentence ‘had six wives’, and the start of the next, ‘The first was...’ etc. Give each pupil in the class a domino at random then see if the class can go through the whole chain of dominos, each pupil reading out their card at the right time. If anyone hesitates the whole class has to start again! This is a nice activity for revising the key points on topics and one that engages a whole class.

There is a free piece of software on the Internet that speeds up the process of making domino cards (and jigsaw style puzzles too) called *Formulator Tarsia* made by Hermitech Laboratory and available for download at this link: http://goo.gl/v7LFY. For instructions on how to use the software visit: http://goo.gl/kkGSi.

Idea 96- Just the first letter

If there are particular phrases that you want your pupils to know then create a puzzle where you just give them the first letter of each word and they have to guess the sentence. For example, 'Angles in a triangle add up to one hundred and eighty degrees' would appear in the puzzle as 'aiatautohaed'. If you want to make it harder, create puzzles where you give them the second letter rather than first.

Idea 97- Running dictation

Put pupils in groups of two or three. On a sheet of paper write all the things you want the pupils to remember. For each group, give them one of these sheets and get them to stick it to the wall, just hanging from the top, with the content facing the wall. One person in each group is the 'scribe' and sits on the other side of the room to their sheet with a blank piece of paper and a pen. The goal of the task is for the scribe to make an exact copy of what is on their sheet of paper on the wall. The non-scribe(s) in the group then have to be the 'messengers' going backwards and forwards between the sheet of paper on the wall and the scribe, communicating the content and layout of the information to the scribe. Pupils seem to really like this one!

Idea 98- White sheet up on the wall

This idea is similar to the *augmented reality* technology that is sweeping through the smartphone market at the moment. The idea of augmented reality is that you view a virtual world imposed onto your own. So for example you walk down the street looking at your phone which is showing what the camera can see. On the screen pops up a review of the restaurant that your phone is passing by or a virtual signpost telling you the way to the nearest bus stop. A virtual world gets overlaid onto the real one.

Since smart phones aren't allowed in exams, how about a bit of 'old fashioned' augmented reality? If your pupils are doing lots of mind-mapping for their revision they will be attempting to stare at a white piece of paper and memorise all the colourful content on it. If your exam boards allow it, why not put a large white sheet up at the front of the exam hall and tell the pupils to 'project their mind-map onto it' using their 'mind's eye'. It sounds crazy but I have read of schools who do this and the pupils say they find it helpful.

Idea 99- Getting to bed a good time

Sleep is vital for learning. Pupils need to know this. If they stay up late and don't get a lot of sleep, much of what they 'learned' yesterday will be wasted. You need REM deep sleep to consolidate your learning and pupils, particularly those getting stressed out around exam time need to ensure they are getting both good quality and a sufficient quantity of sleep. Explain the importance of 'wind down time' and how staring at a back-lit computer screen does not help your brain prepare for sleep. Perhaps suggest some reading from a non-back-lit screen as a good habit for pupils to get into just before bed.

Idea 100- Pupils write each other's tests

To be able to write an assessment you need to understand a topic well. Get your pupils to revise their knowledge by writing tests! If they each do one on a particular topic they can then give it to a partner to take. Make them go through the process of marking what their partner answered. Encourage a conversation between the test maker and the test taker about whether they think their test has been marked fairly and why.

There are lots more things you can do with this model of learning such as getting pupils to pass the tests around the room and choose which one they thought contained the best questions and why. Then can then read peoples' answers on different tests and make corrections if they think they need to. This whole process can lead to a very interesting class discussion if you ask pupils if they are uncertain about anything after completing this work.

~***~

One at a Time

The principle goal of education is to create men and women who are capable of doing new things, not simply repeating what other generations have done.

Jean Piaget

Next time you feel stale and boring as a teacher, as we all do now and again, I hope you find something in this book to help you reinvent yourself and get your enthusiasm flowing again. Whatever you do, don't try to do it all at once and don't fall into the trap of thinking that all good teachers are doing all these things all the time. Everything that I've recommended in this book I learned by watching and chatting to great teachers. Not one of them does anywhere near everything in this book. You can try as many practical strategies to improve the learning in your classroom as you like from this book, but never underestimate the huge importance of developing a rapport and good working relationship with your pupils. Books can't teach that and it's what makes many of the very best teachers so good. If your pupils are still 'with you', wanting to learn even when your lesson has gone pear shaped and the lesson plan has gone out of the window, it is a good sign.

I'd like to finish off this book by giving every teacher who is pure of heart out there a virtual pat on the back. You don't get one very often yet you do one of the most important jobs in the world. Nobody ever forgets a good teacher and whilst your influence in a child's life may not reap rewards until later in their life, I promise if you could really see it, you'd be surprised at the difference you make every day.

Most people do not think that they could be a lawyer, a dentist, a doctor or an accountant. Yet everyone thinks they can teach. One to one tuition is easy to give but you have skills and knowledge just as honed and refined as all the professions above. You can teach a mixed-ability class, stretching each pupil irrespective of ability. You know when to use a reprimand and when to use encouragement to get a pupil back on task. You know how to prevent behavioural issues from happening in the first place so you never have to react to them. You know many different ways of explaining the things you teach and which way is appropriate for the pupils sitting in front of you at that moment. You know how to take a class of hormone-filled teenagers in from a wet and windy lunchtime and have them all working and learning within ten minutes. You are a highly skilled professional that many people fail to appreciate. The job does not bring with it much thanks and yet you keep on starting fresh everyday believing that you can change lives for the better. Good for you!

One of the best pieces of advice I was ever given when I started teaching was:

You'll find this job tough and won't get any thanks for the excellent work you do. Always be nicer to yourself than you think you should be.

Thank you for reading this book and I hope you found it interesting and useful. I'd love to hear from you if you'd like to share your thoughts with me about the book or teaching in general. Feel free to email me on williamgeorgeemeny@gmail.com and/or join my Google+ network at https://plus.google.com/u/0/111288446773159834123/about. If you'd like to follow my maths teaching blog please visit http://www.greatmathsteachingideas.com.

Happy teaching :-)

~***~

6950751R00085

Printed in Great Britain
by Amazon.co.uk, Ltd.,
Marston Gate.